Management: Principles and Policy

Management:
Principles and Policy

A revision aid

Colin Carnall and Susan Maxwell

ICSA Publishing · Cambridge

Published by ICSA Publishing Limited,
Fitzwilliam House, 32 Trumpington Street,
Cambridge CB2 1QY, England

First published 1988

British Library Cataloguing in Publication Data
Carnall, C. A. (Colin A)
   Management.
   1. Management
   I. Title   II. Maxwell, Susan
   658

ISBN 0-902197-59-2

Designed by Geoff Green
Typeset by Pentacor Ltd , High Wycombe, Bucks
Printed in Great Britain by A. Wheaton & Co. Ltd, Exeter

Contents

Preface

This revision aid is designed for students preparing for professional examinations in management, in particular for the Institute of Chartered Secretaries and Administrators. It is divided into two parts. Part One reviews the key learning points and provides an exercise for each of the ten chapters in the companion text (Carnall, Colin, and Maxwell, Susan, *Management: Principles and Policy*, ICSA Publishing Limited, 1988). This is provided to help students plan their reading of the text and their revision. The introductions to the chapters in the companion text are repeated in this revision aid. Part One also reviews the case studies included in that text.

Part Two focuses upon the case study approach which will help students deal with management problems and assist them in developing a logical approach to any question they might tackle in an examination or at work. The chapter on the case study method outlines a simple version of how to approach a case study, which is then applied to a case study. Chapter 12 uses this approach to analyse a case study drawn from an ICSA Management: Principles and Policy paper. Chapter 13 is an implementation exercise which provides a structural approach to setting out a planned set of recommendations and implementation guidelines for a case study. The next three chapters set out analyses of further case studies drawn from ICSA Management: Principles and Policy papers. The final section provides some useful guidance on revision and examination techniques.

Colin A. Carnall
Susan Maxwell

PART ONE

Review of the main learning points

CHAPTER 1

Management work and managerial performance

In today's world, managers face complex and changing pressures and opportunities. On the one hand they must ensure the efficient use of resources. At the same time they must ensure the longer term effectiveness of the organisation for which they work. Effectiveness in a changing environment includes being able to identify the right things to do in the future (the right products and services to offer, appropriate technologies, procedures and structures, and people with appropriate skills) and ensuring the flexibility and adaptability necessary for change to be achieved.

Implementing change effectively has been, and seems likely to remain, one of the main challenges facing managers. In both the private and public sector, in manufacturing, banking, health care and education, this challenge is presented, often in very stark circumstances. Sales and profitability may be falling rapidly. A merger bid may lead managers to review performance and plans as part of a defence. De-regulation causes dramatic changes in many sectors. Central government expenditure pressures can create serious constraints in the public sector, often with dramatic effects on budgets. Privatisation and competitive tendering have led many organisations to develop greater commercial awareness and disciplines amongst their staff. Managers are concerned about value for money, the development and marketing of new products and services, flexibility, whether of design, manufacture or service delivery, or in organisational structure and management style.

Managers are increasingly concerned about product/service performance and quality. Customers and clients are ever more vocal and critical. This applies across the whole spectrum of organisations. Automobile manufacturers use quality and reliability as a selling feature of cars. In education we talk of 'parent involvement' and 'parent power'.

The main focus of management is switching from internal concerns to a balanced focus upon both internal and external matters. This book is concerned with the management of enterprises internally (organisation structures, managerial effectiveness, motivation, coping with change) and externally (planning and implementing new strategies, managing corporate affairs and image).

Key learning points

1. Sources of ineffectiveness

In organisations there is a need for people to take views and positions which discourage further enquiry. This situation arises when, for example, a significant change in policy is made and people who feel left out from the decision-making process wish to question the decision. Negative feelings are suppressed in an attempt to diffuse conflict and reduce criticism. People have a tendency to appear rational and argue points in what appears to be logical and realistic ways. In part this is to save upsetting others but, it must also be borne in mind that during meetings people want to control proceedings in a way which maximises winning. By minimising expression of negative feelings an expression of being rational is maintained.

This desire to keep things logical and rational can on the surface appear to be effective. However, these behaviours can fog issues especially when valid information is needed or people are dealing with difficult and threatening problems. If these issues are not dealt with to the individual's satisfaction, then they can create contradictions and lead to crisis situations. Performance and motivation can be severely affected when issues are suppressed and individuals feel they are not being listened to. This can, and does, lead to organisations becoming ineffective as they become demotivated which affects performance. Managers who are too busy to devote time to properly communicating to subordinates may indirectly contribute to ineffectiveness.

Ineffectiveness is both the enemy of, and the target of, efforts to achieve change. Ineffectiveness makes it difficult to generate the commitment needed to change effectively. Changes within organisations need to be implemented in ways which make the people working within that organisation feel they will improve the work situation for them. Thus, people will work with change and not against it, reduce conflict which may inhibit effectiveness and this, in turn, will lead to greater effectiveness for the organisation.

2. Leadership and excellence

Another way of considering change is thinking about management culture. Many writers suggest that 'excellent' companies – those which are effective – can emerge from organisational cultures which encourage the following:

Accountability
This refers to direct and personal accountability for performance. The stress is upon the individual manager for the performance of his* team.

Synergy
Getting co-operation and collaboration. Much work demands the efforts of a variety of people from a variety of technical disciplines. This means managing the process of getting things done by co-operation.

Cross cultural skills
Working with people from diverse backgrounds often within large public sector services or multi-national corporations.

Managing interfaces
Co-ordinating the deployment of people, information resources,

---

* Throughout this book the masculine term is used purely as a stylistic convenience and in all cases can equally mean the feminine.

etc. in order to establish the smooth running of effective organisations.

Financial realism
Taking financial issues properly into account along with other issues such as technical or marketing factors.

3. *Managerial performance*

Managerial performance is a combination of knowledge and skill applied in practice. Managerial work is characterised by variety and fragmentation. Trivial and important issues are mixed and generate continual change. Managers have little time to devote to any particular issue and so spend time dealing with current and specific problems. He has many roles to play within his job. His is the figure-head of the organisation, leader of a team, liaison person with senior management, contractor, client and supplier. He processes data and transmits information, becoming the nerve centre of the organisation. He monitors the organisation so that he understands what is taking place in order to build knowledge and make decisions. He channels information outside the organisation about the organisation. He allocates resources and handles the everyday disturbances within his team. So, the manager's performance is contingent upon many factors and needs to combine skill and knowledge in order to deal effectively with the demands of his role.

4. *The managerial job*

In order to apply the skills and knowledge needed for managerial performance to maximum effectiveness, managers must acquire self-knowledge and insight in order to develop a thorough understanding of the managerial job as a whole. Managers must know how to communicate the many levels of information to diverse receivers and use their power and authority with discretion.

The managerial job is both complex and demanding. Managers always have opportunities to improve effectiveness, efficiency, etc. whatever their level within the organisation but this needs initiative to generate constructive change. This book is concerned with understanding what managers can actually do to achieve progress for their organisation through improvement and change.

Exercise

Consider the four key learning points, described in this chapter, in the light of your own experience at work. Which areas can be improved in relation to what you have learned and how could this be achieved?

CHAPTER 2

Managerial accountability

Managers are responsible for the work of other people. In effect a manager is authorised (either by mandates from his Board of Directors, or through a formal job description) to delegate work to his or her staff. When a supervisor examines a manager's accountability for the quality of the work performed by a subordinate, there are two basic considerations, as follows:

1. The manager must be able to decide what tasks will be delegated to the subordinate, and what resources will be allocated to the subordinate to carry out those tasks.
2. The manager cannot properly be accountable for the work of a subordinate who in the manager's judgement is below the level of competence necessary for getting the delegated work done.

In this context, the authority attached to a managerial position gives the right to exercise power within socially established limits. In many instances, the right extends to applying positive or negative sanctions (rewards or punishment) to subordinates, depending upon the quality of their performance behaviour. However, in practice, this does not work in a straightforward sense. Managers are expected to develop and train their staff and therefore, in practice, (2) above is rather 'fluid'.

How managers are authorised to have power is an important question. In many countries legislation influences the way in which public and private sector enterprises are run, causing variations between countries and political systems. In a democracy of the kind found in Britain and North America, the power of the government is authorised by the group of electors towards whom the power is being used, thereby making that power legitimate. Indirectly, this also applies to companies in the private sector, governed by the constraints built into company law, employment law and so on. These laws give certain powers to employers which permit, within limits, the exercise of power over their managers and employees. Similarly, the directors of a company are obliged to control the company in the best interests of the shareholders. However, therein lies a number of issues regarding the efficacy of shareholder control (see Thomas, 1973). Power, however, should not be seen purely as the right to apply sanctions to others. In practice, it is the quality of individuals or groups which enables them to influence the behaviour of other individuals (singly or collectively) in such a way that those with influence are helped to fulfil their own aims. It is the quality of a manager that gets others to act, to work, and to carry out activities on his behalf. Thus the sources of power will include the professional and personal credibility of the manager concerned.

Key learning points

1. The operational core and its organisation

The operational core is that part of the enterprise which directly produces outputs involving the development of goods or services, their production and their presentation to clients, or a market, for sale or delivery. The character of these will vary according to the organisation. For example, research, design and development tasks are concerned with modifying products or developing new products. Therefore, these tasks are organised into departments concerned with developing the same or related products. We must also examine the organisation of activities provided in support of operational activities. These involve a wide range of lateral relationships with differing degrees of accountability and authority.

2. Prescribing relationships

Relationships are prescribed according to the competence of the person performing the work. If performance falls below the accepted standard then the matter might be taken up by his or her superior for the latter to discuss with a more senior person. Professional staff are typical examples of prescribing relationships. The professional head retains accountability and authority for other members of his team. A variation of this theme can be where the same specialism provides expertise at two levels, e.g. accountancy at head office and subsidiary level. This arrangement typifies 'functional organisations' where decentralisation is being introduced.

3. Roles and relationships

To co-ordinate the work of subordinates in a large enterprise, a manager may need specialised assistance. This is a different role from a supervisor who deals with many aspects of the manager's work. The staff specialist concentrates on only one aspect of work, e.g. the relationship of a planner and a programmer. Monitoring performance is an important role in accountability. Monitoring involves checking that the activities of employees of the organisation conform to standards. The monitor needs authority to perform his role along with knowledge of the activity, e.g. the role of inspector.

In a co-ordinating role the person concerned is accountable for co-ordinating the activities of others in some defined task. Such a role might include producing a report on the implementation of a project. The co-ordinator will monitor progress and have authority to propose action, arrange meetings and in cases of disagreement, go directly to those who set the task.

4. Demands, constraints and choices

According to Stewart (1970) work can be analysed into three categories: demands, constraints and choices. Demands are what a manager must do. Constraints are the factors both internal and external to the organisation that limit what a manager can do. Choices are activities that the manager can, but not necessarily has to do. These represent opportunities to managers, not problems. If a difficulty arises it is a manager's opportunity to employ his managerial skills to achieve an effective result.

Some unit areas of operation offer scope for choice when the output is not clearly prescribed. Thus, more scope exists in staff and service jobs, in some sales jobs or subsidiary management posts. Choice may also exist in work sharing between manager and subordinates. Obviously the latter needs to be skilled and knowledgeable. This can occur in a marketing function when a senior manager travels abroad and needs someone to deputise in his absences. Constraints which organisations impose on their managers and subordinates are the logical consequence of relating the authority of individuals to their accountability. Accountability is of key importance in modern management practices.

Exercise

Consider what you have learned about accountability with regard to roles and responsibility within an organisation.

CHAPTER 3

Manager motivation and development

The design of organisation structures to suit the needs of the particular business enterprise or organisation, providing for the co-ordination of the diverse activities carried out within the enterprise or organisation, but also providing for adaptability to respond to changing circumstances, presents a challenge to management which cannot be overstated in importance. The structure of an organisation allows the pursuit of objectives and the implementation of plans. People and resources are allocated to the tasks which must be performed, and co-ordination is provided. Working methods, rules and procedures define the ways in which tasks are to be performed and/or establish criteria for task performance, output or quality. These are typically all related to reward systems, planning and scheduling systems and monitoring systems. The aspects of the structure of an organisation are articulated in the information system.

Moreover, the structure of the organisation provides a decision support system. Arrangements are made for the collection and processing of information relevant to the decisions managers make. Specialist posts are often created to provide for such arrangements. Accountants and organisation and methods personnel will, for example, collect and process information on various aspects of the performance of the organisation. This information will be evaluated and presented to decision makers either regularly (to a senior management meeting) or in response to particular circumstances (for example, when a major contract becomes open for bids). The tasks of the organisation create decisions to be made. In practice decision makers decide that certain tasks will be undertaken and others not, from the range of tasks which could be undertaken, for which a market exists. For a decision system to be effective, provisions for monitoring trends in the market are essential. Changes in technology, in resource markets for capital or labour and in the product market will affect the performance of any organisation requiring adaptation.

Key learning points

1. Contingency theory

Contingency theory is based on the assumption that there is no 'best way' to design an organisation structure but, instead, the effectiveness of the design of a particular organisation is contingent upon various factors. These will be based upon technology, the environment and the history of the organisation, the norms, expectations and size of the organisation. The theory suggests that organisational performance depends upon the extent to which the organisation secures a good match between situation and structure.

2. Theories of motivation

There is no one guiding principle which governs what motivates people. What will motivate in one set of circumstances may not in another. Effective motivation needs to take into account the needs of the organisation and the needs of the individual within the organisation. There are five main theories considered appropriate, which are as follows:

Equity theory
People compare themselves with appropriate others and judge whether or not they are fairly treated. Dissatisfaction will result if they perceive they are not treated fairly in contrast to others.

Achievement
Some people are achievement orientated and strive for excellence through competitive situations. Most people have a degree of

achievement orientation but this may vary according to early childhood experiences. If independence and performance are a high priority within the family then a high need to achieve is usually exhibited. Achievement orientation appears to work well in situations which are challenging and competitive and which require a high level of performance.

Self-actualisation
Some psychologists have studied the importance of human needs in relation to work. Maslow (1954) developed a hierarchical model of motivation which springs from needs which are not satisfied. Once one need is satisfied it is replaced by another. This gradually develops until the individual self-actualises and reaches his own level of satisfaction from the work performed. Managers have a high desire to self-actualise as they seek challenge and promotion.

Herzberg's two factor theory
The two factor theory distinguishes that satisfying and dissatisfying are independent factors of work. The theory suggests that different parts of the job will influence feelings of satisfaction and dissatisfaction. Therefore a person can feel satisfied with some parts of a job whilst feeling dissatisfied with others. Self-actualising and two factor theory distinguish intrinsically motivating features and can influence job design and concern for worker satisfaction.

Expectancy theory
Looks at both individual and environmental factors to explain motivation. People are seen to have different needs and to seek different outcomes from work. These choices will depend upon their perceptions of the likelihood that a particular behaviour will lead to a desired outcome.

3. Motivation and its impact on work

The way work is arranged can provide opportunities for individuals to experience increased satisfaction. How this is done depends upon the type of job and organisation, and the design of the job is a crucial variable in determining the types of reward it supplies.

4. Career planning and development

Career development requires planning in order that it may be successful. Career planning can be achieved by goal setting. These goals may be expressed in long and short term needs. To facilitate this process some features need to be fulfilled – accurate self assessment, skills assessment, identification of strengths and weaknesses. We also need a realistic examination of organisations to develop goals which are achievable. Career development is a two way process. It requires individual career management to be placed within the context of organisational factors.

The design for career planning can be broadly defined into three stages, as follows:
1. Define work activities.
2. Identify personal requirements.
3. Recognise job families.

Career paths also need to be identified within organisations. This information may be formally available in some organisations or informally through the process of networking with appropriate others.

5. Management development

Management development can mean different things in different organisations. Managers need to develop specific skills and organisations need to harness these skills towards achieving their goals. Leadership skills are an integral and essential part of a manager's role. Therefore, management development is not one single component but part of an integrated whole. Management development programmes can increase skills and competency in managers through careful planning and a systematic approach. Programmes for management development are likely to include the following:
(a) In house training – training carried out within the organisation.
(b) External training – sending managers outside the organisation to appropriate courses.

(c)   Job rotation – this can broaden job experience and increase the manager's sensitivity in appreciating the problems of others.

(d)   Secondments – temporary assignments to other organisations.

(e)   Mentoring – senior managers assisting subordinates to grow into new jobs.

(f)   Project groups – setting up different inter departmental groups to work on organisational problems.

This chapter considered, as one grouping, motivation, career development and management development. They have been examined together because in the world of management problems they overlap extensively. A problem in any one area often leads to problems in the other two.

Exercise

Describe and analyse the differences between career development and management development. Draw up a career plan of your own identifying long and short term goals and what steps you need to take in order to achieve them.

CHAPTER 4

Organisation design

It has been recognised for some time that the structure an organisation develops has an influence on a range of matters such as the ability of top managers to give effect to their decisions, the discretion available to middle managers and the ability of management to motivate employees. It thus influences enterprise performance.

A manager in a service industry has prepared for an expected throughput of work following the introduction of a new financial investment scheme. Fortunately for the company, but unfortunately for his department, the Marketing Department's forecasts are wildly wrong. The actual throughput is 500 per cent above the expected level. The manager needs to urgently obtain extra premises, staff, equipment, etc. To exploit this 'opportunity' he needs to break through the restrictions of the conventional structure and obtain increased budgets from the Accounting Department, staff recruitment through the Personnel Department, move equipment via the Computer Department and move furniture via the Premises Department. The formal organisation structure prevents the manager from having all the resources he needs to deal with the situation under his direct control.

By organisation structure we mean the relationship between the different parts of the organisation. Organisations may be said to have the following characteristics:

1. They are composed of people and groups of people.
2. They are purposeful, goal-oriented social instruments.

3.   They apply various means in order to accomplish objec-
      tives. There are two such means often seen as essential to
      goal achievement:
      (a)   Differentiation of functions and positions; and
      (b)   Rational, planned attempts to co-ordinate and
            direct activities.
4.   The activities and relationships within organisations may
      be conceived of as continuous through time and chang-
      ing in so far as organisations grow, decline and change,
      and people are promoted or dismissed, leave, or retire,
      and new people are appointed. (Porter and Lawler, 1975)

Traditionally, organisations have been described as systems of
formal authority using an organisatonal chart, such as that
shown in Fig. 4.1.

The organisation chart provides a controversial picture of an
organisation and many do not possess a formal written-down
chart. Many people argue that an organisation chart is misleading
in that many important relationships of authority, communication or co-operation cannot be shown on such a chart. Nevertheless, an organisation chart provides a means of showing:

1.   The position which exists in an organisation.
2.   How the various positions are grouped into units (in Fig.
      4.1, design, installation and quality are grouped into the
      engineering department).
3.   How formal authority flows among them.

Formal authority is only one aspect of an organisation. In
practice organisations function in far more complex ways. Behaviour within an organisation includes a considerable amount
of activity outside the formal systems of authority and communication often referred to as the informal organisation. We, the
authors, define organisation structure as follows: 'the structure of
relationships, procedures and arrangements which constitutes
the organisation of an enterprise.' The relationships involved are
those arising from the distribution of authority and influence and
the allocation of duties within the enterprise. The procedures and
arrangements refer to the means employed to organise and
control work.

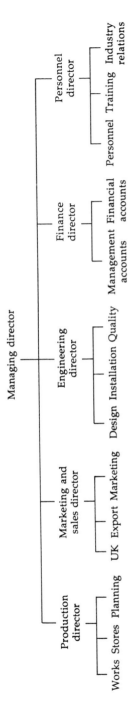

Fig. 4.1 A typical organisation chart.

Key learning points

1. Bureaucracy

This is the most often referred to type of organisation. There is, however, a difference between the bureaucractic model and bureaucracy as practiced. As a form of organisation, bureaucracy allows enterprises to transcend the limits of direct control by the owners or by charismatic individuals. For this to be effective three pre-conditions must be met, as follows:

(a).   The number of hierarchical levels must be low allowing direct communication and face to face supervision.

(b).   Tasks need to be performed within a restricted geographical area. This allows people in control to visit regularly.

(c).   The range and diversity of functions must be low. All members need to be involved in broadly the same area.

Bureaucratic organisations are characterised by high levels of specialisation and differentiation between jobs and departments by several layers of management, by standardisation of procedures and by formalisation. We can distinguish between the recognised two types of bureaucracy, as follows:

Mechanistic bureaucracy.
This emphasises power of rules and specific standards.

Professional bureaucracy.
Here individuals are socialised into particular patterns of behaviour through long training. The professional bureaucracy tends to be decentralised. Professionals do their own work and seek collective control on administrative decisions, whereas the mechanistic bureaucracy emphasises direct control and constant checking by supervisors.

2. Matrix structures

Matrix structures combine both functional and project organisation structures. Individuals have membership of two groups – a specialist department (functional) and a cross disciplinary team. Matrix structures can be either temporary or enduring. Temporary means they are only established for the life of a particular project. Matrix structures have advantages and disadvantages, as follows:

Advantages include:
- Clear project objectives.
- Co-ordination across functional lines.
- Efficient use of resources.
- Retention of teams of functional experts beyond the life of a particular project.
- Information flow is improved.
- Development of general management through project management post.

Disadvantages include:
- Complexity which such structures can create.
- Difficulties in establishing priorities.
- Potential conflict of individuals with varying interests.

3. The development of multi-national organisations

Large organisations have needed to develop administrative structures and professional, managerial competence to ensure continuity and deal with complex activities. To do this success-fully a complex set of resources needs to be co-ordinated. The growth, size and complexity of functions of these enterprises creates pressure on the people managing them. When an enter-prise adds a new product to its range diversification, it often hires new people with appropriate skills and expertise. A new depart-ment with specific responsibility for this product will be estab-lished. Existing procedures may not cope appropriately with the demands of the new product and problems such as these can lead to conflict between departments and absorb the time of senior management.

4. The multi-divisional form and its problems

Diversification may lead to divisionalisation and encourage efficient allocation of capital and other resources thus providing greater opportunities for management development. However, this can cause problems in innovation. Innovation does not thrive under central control. Control systems used by divisionalised firms to minimise risk and co-ordinate efforts may militate against new ideas.

5. New technology

Changes caused by new technology are a major challenge to management today, and have an impact on the role of middle management too. Divisional staff is often streamlined and management accountability becomes greater. Information systems allow more direct control of key issues, e.g. finance, performance from the centre.

6. Control systems

Monitoring performance via ﬁn feedback is an important part of the management task, and is related to motivation. If, however, targets are set for control, performance assessment and incentive payment then staff may wish to lower them in order to allow for a greater chance of success. Most large organisations attempt to overcome such problems by setting budgets participatively and through extensive performance appraisal dealing with performance and future plans for improvement.

7. Organisation design and its complexity

Organisation design, it is obvious to see, is not a precise science. However, issues such as control, resources and the environment are important features of organisation design. Lawrence (1983) argues that organisation designs are related to the complexity of the environment and scarcity of resources for the organisation. He identifies appropriate organisation forms for each combination of information complexity and resource scarcity. Information complexity refers to the diversity of, uncertainty about, and range of technologies and opportunities in the organisation's environment. In practice, organisations attempt to control their environments to some degree. However, we need to remember that the environment in which the organisation operates and the adaptation of general management are both crucial issues.

In this section we have examined some concepts and approaches to organisation design. The practical implications of this will be examined in later chapters.

Exercise

What organisation structure does your company have? Can you obtain an organisation chart? How effective is the structure?

CHAPTER 5

Developing corporate strategy

To develop a corporate organisation we need to be able to 'stand back' and take a 'broad view'. We must learn to see the organisation as a whole. Crucially we must be able to generate a 'vision of the future'. What business are we in? What are the main strategic threats and opportunities? What major changes in the environment are likely to have an effect on the organisation in the next few years? These are amongst the questions to which we must try to get reasonably objective answers.

The need for good strategic thinking in today's world is clear enough and has been discussed already. The pace of change in technology, market conditions and in political and cultural conditions presents real challenges. To acquire or divest activities. To enter or withdraw from markets. To restructure, redesign, automate production. To diversify or to concentrate on core businesses. These are all key decisions which will have an important effect on the economic well-being of the organisation.

Key learning points

1. Corporate objectives

Corporate objectives will vary according to the culture and structure of the organisation. Planning specific goals and seeming to act with precision may not always be a good thing. This could create a view that nothing can be changed, creating an atmosphere which stifles ideas and initiative. Specific objectives may encourage those who feel opposed to them to unite against them and cause conflict within the organisation. It can also provide valuable information to competitors, particularly if senior managers move. But, what kind of objectives do managers pursue? This is often talked about in terms of profitability, survival and growth though in practice this means maintaining independence. This, as many argue, is a spur for effectiveness but it must also be remembered that it is time consuming and sets only short term priorities.

Strategic planning is a process of identifying different businesses or service areas within which the organisation is and should be operating. It needs to identify critical factors for success and find methods of ensuring that success. Literature on this subject provides us with some useful guidelines, as follows:

(a)   Lead from success.
(b)   Concentrate resources where you have competitive advantages.
(c)   Concentrate on narrow product/market scope at unit level.
(d)   Invest in future earning power.

A useful pair of concepts for strategic planning are the learning curve and progress functions. The argument is that with high production volumes costs fall for various reasons. It is possible to plot unit cost against accumulative volume on a log scale and get a straight line relationship (see Fig. 4.1, in chapter 4). The experience curve is a function of; product improvement, technological change, and economies of scale.

More complex models exist but some techniques carry the danger of being overly scientific. Whilst they are useful they should not be allowed to dominate strategy formulation.

2. Basic steps in corporate planning

There are two main basic steps in corporate planning, as follows:

Corporate appraisal.
Finance, personnel, management facilities/technology, markets and products.

Environmental appraisal.
Economic, social/political, technological and competitive. Appraisal leads to the development of strategy through judgement and creativity. From this approach operational plans, annual plans, budgets and reviews can be established. Systems do not create effective plans, people do! Yet we need systems to help us effect our plans.

3. Corporate planning

The 1980s have become the era of strategic management. Concern is with both the development and implementation of strategy. Business and corporate leadership are now important. Management of change is crucial. New challenges reside in achieving effective changes to the organisation's corporate culture.

4. Competitive analysis

According to Porter (1980, 1985) the intensity of competition within any industry is determined by basic competitive forces. The strength of these determines the long run profit potential of the industry. These forces include the threat of new entrants, competition, substitution (effective ceiling on price), bargaining power of buyers and suppliers. In order to develop relevant intelligence on these, many sources of relevant data must be researched and the results utilised. This will apply both outside and inside the company. The greater the use of such scenarios, the wider the range of strategic options which need to be considered.

Corporate strategy also needs to be modified to match the conditions of world trade. In a *laissez faire* environment producers may continue to export from their home base. If conditions are more protectionalist they will be able to obtain access to national markets only if they manufacture or assemble their products locally.

Plans are only of use if they are implemented. The discipline of corporate planning can contribute to manager development but planning will only contribute to the growth and/or the development of the organisation if implementation follows.

Exercise

What issues need to be considered in corporate planning? Consider the strengths and weaknesses in 'formal' corporate plans.

CHAPTER 6

Conditions for effective change

We have seen that change is one of the key management tasks and responsibilities today. Whether it be in response to market, technological or social forces, the role of the manager is to ensure that changes are introduced effectively. To do so requires the understanding of three essential points.

First, change creates anxiety. Significant changes to an organisation are costly, time-consuming and require energy and motivation on the part of those concerned. Only if people recognise the need for change, and can see the prospect of improvement, are they likely to feel the impetus to invest the energy and commitment needed. Change creates opportunities for the organisation as a whole, and for individual employees. Second, change requires careful planning and implementation. People must be briefed, teams formed, resources made available, objectives set, progress reviewed and so on. All of this demands careful programming. Only by doing so can we identify the problems which may arise, and any particular pressure points.

Finally, change and conflict are closely linked. No significant organisational change can be introduced without some conflict. Managers will hold different views about what needs doing to improve an organisation. Determined and effective managers are likely to push those views forcibly. Thus there will always be organisational politics and conflict associated with change. As we shall see it is important for us to understand these politics and then learn how to manage the politics of change in order that they turn out to be constructive.

Thus for effective organisational change to be possible there must exist the capacity to handle anxiety, to develop workable and acceptable plans and to manage conflict constructively. In the next section we will turn to three views of what comprises an effective or innovative organisation. In effect we argue that effective change requires effective organisation in the first place. In offering this argument we accept the commonly used distinction between efficiency and effectiveness as follows:

1. Efficiency

Means that we achieve the objectives we have already, in terms of say cost, quality, resources and so on.

2. Effectiveness

Includes efficiency and, adaptability; the effective organisation is one which is able to achieve its main objectives efficiently *and* adapt to significantly changing circumstances in its market place.

Argyris (1964) defines three core activities of any organisation as follows:

1. Achieving objectives.
2. Maintaining the internal system.
3. Adapting to the external environment.

'Achieving objectives' relates to the direct accomplishment of objectives – for example meeting delivery dates, quality, standards and so on. 'Maintaining the internal system' includes all the formal activities of authority and control including training, budgets, communication and rewards. 'Adapting to the external environment' includes marketing, product development, public and community relations. Effective organisations will be those achieving an appropriate balance between the three core activities. The balance needed will clearly be influenced by the rate of change the organisation is experiencing, both internally and externally, but more of that later.

Key learning points

Change requires effective organisation for it to be successful. It needs to be both efficient – achieving the objectives set, and effective – adaptable in order to achieve its objectives and adapt to changing circumstances as they occur.

1. The innovative organisation

An organisation needs to be innovative. It must focus on its own performance in getting things done, on concentrating its strengths, on centralising key issues such as finance, whilst decentralising implementation and allowing middle level managers the autonomy they need to perform effectively.

Organisational development literature has interesting points to make about what makes an organisation effective. Rickards (1985) identifies key issues in deciding a strategy for innovation. These include the following:

(a)   Innovation is systematic because all factors are inter-related; social, economic, political, technological, cultural and commercial.

(b)   Innovation is non-linear. It stops and starts and is often accidental (e.g. the discovery of penicillin).

(c)   Innovation is problem solving and requires imagination and flexibility.

(d)   Innovation is situational. There is no one 'best' way.

(e)   Innovation requires structure.

(f)   Innovation is mission-orientated, requiring impetus high visibility and success.

(g)   Innovation requires negotiation and participation which in turn can produce conflict.

(h)   Innovation is personal and global. It involves and affects individuals and communities.

All these suggest an active role for management in defining structures, tasks, project teams and in publicising success and providing necessary support. In essence, innovation both is and requires organisational change. To launch a new product or service is itself to achieve change, but to create the conditions for this innovation we need to achieve flexibility and organisational effectiveness.

2. Organisational culture

For change to be effective the organisational culture needs to be adaptable. Local management needs some autonomy in order to make its own decisions around issues such as reward systems. Knowledge needs to be broadened around specialist/professional boundaries. There needs to be a climate where openness is encouraged so problems can be dealt with directly. Communication needs to be improved through management information systems and simplified procedures. Task team approaches at local level will increase professional development as we mentioned in Chapter 3 of the companion text. 'Power culture' within the organisation is another important aspect of organisational culture. This is particularly evident in small, growing companies where organisations are highly dependent on strong leadership. Here control is exercised from the centre and decisions are made largely as an outcome of influence rather than rationality. An organisation such as this can react well to change but having a high level of quality in its top people is crucial. Culture is not only an internal issue but also an external one too. In today's business world we find ourselves working more and more often with people from different occupational, local and national cultures. Effective management thus demands the capacity to deal with cross cultural issues and influences. We need to build empathy to manage this effectively. In a changing world we need to develop a realistic view of both internal and external forces, understand the company's problems and seek out ways to develop solutions.

3. Learning from change

Change involves learning. If problems and solutions are discussed openly and if constructive attitudes to change prevail, then significant change can be achieved. Learning is achieved from exploring dilemmas and by experimentation. People need to understand problems and need to be brought into the process of seeking solutions. Learning involves risk taking and a climate which promotes trying out new ideas. In order to learn we need to examine personal beliefs and conflicts. Only by doing this can we free ourselves to be open to new ideas. We must also recognise the value of other peoples' attitudes and ideas. Management styles must be adaptive to encourage individuals rather than block discussion and creativity.

If we wish to achieve change we must move from the present

state to the desired and planned for future. We can build upon strengths as part of our approach to manage change, using the process of change to deal with weaknesses and using the learning which is associated with change. But more is needed to achieve change. We must involve skills and ideas from outside sources to improve on weaknesses. This will demonstrate that management is committed to improvement both for the company and those who work within it.

Exercise

Using force field analysis as described in Chapter 6 of the companion text, select a situation you are familiar with that requires change. List both strengths and weaknesses that this change involves and try to find realistic ways of building strengths and minimising weaknesses.

CHAPTER 7

Managerial skills for managing change

This chapter draws together ideas on management skills, the management of change and the impact of organisation structures, systems and technologies on people. In Chapter 6 we have considered some of the skills for managing change. Synthesizing these ideas we propose to outline the managerial skills needed for the effective management of change. First we will look at planning change and dealing with the politics of change. We then go on to describe a simple model of how people experience major changes and how we can help them (and ourselves) to cope with significant organisational changes.

Key learning points

1. Blocks to problem solving

In planning change we need to also generate creative solutions to what are essentially novel problems. A framework is needed which will support and encourage creative solutions. To sustain this process we need to examine first the blocks, that prevent us and others from releasing creativity and problem solving, in order that we can understand how to manage this process. An analysis of blocks follows:

Perceptual blocks
We often see what we expect to see and consequently stereotype issues. It is often difficult to extrapolate key issues in problem

solving and consequently we get lost in a mass of problems which seem big and unwieldly. At the same time we could also be too narrow in our thinking around the problem and have invested too much in our own constructions thus ignoring other groups who are affected and could help us view problems from other perspectives which in turn could aid problem solving.

When a problem seems unsolvable, we tend to get swamped by data and become saturated with information. Looking at other organisations who have experienced similar changes and seeing how they tackled issues is a useful exercise though we may not always consider their solutions.

Emotional blocks

Often we are plunged into inertia by fear of risk taking. Risk taking must be based on realism and organisations must be careful not to see lack of success as failure and punish the manager responsible. Solutions are often complex and problem solving is a messy process. This must also be taken into account. Evident in problem solving is also the unwillingness to 'sleep on a problem'. In planning the process of managing change we should plan enough time for ideas to incubate.

Cultural blocks

The culture in which we are raised has a significant impact upon the way we think about problems. Adams (1987) believes that our culture trains out mental playfulness, fantasy and reflectiveness by placing more stress on the value of channelled mental activities. Concurrent with this view is the function of humour in problem solving. Humour is often based on the process of associating apparently unrelated ideas. Creativity is the same – it involves the association of unrelated ideas and structures, and therefore, according to Adams, humour is one ingredient for active problem solving. We harbour beliefs that reason, logic and numbers are constructive and that intuition, feelings and pleasure are counter-productive. This becomes even more profound when we assign these characteristics to sex roles, e.g. men are logical, physical, pragmatic and women are sensitive, emotional and intuitive. Creativity demands a balance of all these characteristics. Other emotional blocks which we find hard to overcome are those we base on tradition. Tradition is important, our commitment and motivation are based on tradition but whilst we must respect the role of tradition, we must also realise the need for change.

Environmental blocks
We have previously mentioned the importance of support during times of change. Change is often seen as threatening, and new ideas are easily stopped and over analysed much too early. Those who generate ideas also have a responsibility to hear criticism from others and so build an atmosphere of trust and support.

Cognitive blocks
Using jargonistic language, e.g. mathematical, professional, can hinder creative problem solving as can inflexible strategies, and lack of correct information can clearly be a limiting factor. Information leads to expertise, which is necessary but thinking only along such lines can close off creative solutions.

2. *Working through blocks*

So far we have identified a number of blocks which can inhibit problem solving. Now we can look at how these blocks can be worked through. Here is a checklist which you may find useful in achieving this:

- Stay fluid in your thinking until rigour is needed.
- Do not criticise new and, perhaps, revolutionary ideas.
- Encourage a think-tank approach.
- Acknowledge good ideas – be approving.
- Eliminate status and rank.
- Be optimistic.
- Be supportive.
- Learn from making mistakes.
- Share risks.
- Build on ideas.
- Do not evaluate too early.

Here are some actions which discourage creativity:

- Heavy criticism too early.
- Being competitive.
- Being pessimistic.
- Pointing out flaws.

- Not listening.
- Being non-committal.
- Anger.
- Being distant.

These are just a few points. A more comprehensive list can be found in your companion text book.

3. *Organisational politics*

To manage change we must understand and handle corporate politics. We need to understand political power bases and how to use them. Understanding and using networks is a key factor. Mentoring can help managers to recognise key staff who can positively influence change. Managers use a variety of resources as they engage in the politcs of organisations. They must use formal authority, by virtue of their position, have direct control over resources and control of information.

4. *Coping with major changes*

Change creates uncertainty, anxiety and stress. It also has an impact on individuals' self esteem and therefore their performance. Change means having to adapt to new ideas, methods, procedures, etc. Let us now look more closely at the mechanisms of coping with change:

Denial
Some people will begin by denying that change is necessary. They may feel overwhelmed by what is going on. New ideas will be rejected and a preference for the 'old ways' will be seen as the 'best ways'. Performance is likely to fall off though we typically see a raise in self-esteem as groups band together against what feels threatening.

Defence
Eventually the recognition that new ways are inevitable pervades. This can lead to feelings of frustration and depression because it can be difficult to deal with these changes. People attempt to defend their own jobs and articulate this through ritualistic behaviour.

Discarding
Now people begin to let go of the past and look forward to the future. We are not sure how this happens but it is clear that appropriate support plays an important role. Optimism grows along with self-esteem. New systems are dealt with through constructive attitudes and there is a spirit of enquiry rather than resistance.

Adaptation
Now a process of mutual adaptation emerges. Individuals begin to test new situations and themselves. By doing so they develop new skills understanding and attachments.

Internalisation
New relationships between people and processes have been tried, modified and accepted. These now become incorporated into understandings of new work situations. New behaviour becomes part of normal behaviour.

In this section we have discussed ways and means of introducing major changes effectively. Here we wish to stress one crucial point. Effective organisations are those which introduce change quickly and in which people, employees and managers learn about the business as this process proceeds. Achieving change without learning is possible, but sometimes not without a struggle, especially if powerful groups oppose the changes. Introducing change in ways which do not encourage learning is likely to entrench negative attitudes to change in the future. Only if people and organisations change, by learning from the experience of change, can effectiveness be achieved and sustained. We have attempted to draw together a range of ideas and practical steps to help people manage change effectively.

Exercise

Using both your own experience and what you have learned about managerial skills for managing change, analyse the key factors for implementing change within an organisation.

CHAPTER 8

Managing through crisis

The 1970s and 1980s have been an era of dramatic change affecting public and private organisations alike. They have also been an era in which companies have failed (that is failed to operate successfully in a marketplace and been liquidated or gone bankrupt) or been contracted as previous levels of activity became unsustainable in one way or another. An early study of the causes and symptoms of 'corporate collapse' was published by Argenti (1976) with a more recent study being that of Kharbanda and Stallworthy (1985). It is clear enough that the onset of failure can be predicted and failure avoided through management actions. A number of such examples have recently generated a new genre of management look – the management of turnaround (Slatter (1984)).

Key learning points

1. Corporate failure

Many factors may contribute to corporate failure and according to Argenti (1977) signals of failure can be observed before the fact thereby allowing prediction. So, what can be done about this? Organisations facing failure problems must look at a number of key challenges. They need to achieve sustainable changes quickly but without the resources available in periods of growth. It is a time to reorganise and rationalise. Difficult decisions must be taken and implemented, products redesigned, processes updated and new skills acquired along with new people. Taylor (1983) believes these challenges require a new style of management. The situation calls for speed and ruthlessness in decision making. Management must rely more on personal face to face meetings and conversations. Greater emphasis must be put on responsibility and accountability; tighter controls on cash. It is a time to re-think the future prospects for each product and market segment e.g. considering international expansion sometimes into politically risky areas. Managers need the ability to negotiate with employee representatives, pressure groups and government bodies both at home and abroad. Firms must adopt and develop new technologies or go under. It is a time of innovation and risk taking.

The key to the problem is to manage the contraction of traditional activities whilst at the same time expanding new activities. This must be achieved quickly and with limited resources, often under pressure and with demotivated staff. Strategies concerned with management of turnaround need to include mergers and co-operative supply sales and assets and programmes aimed at reducing overheads, improved systems of cost and budgetary control, value for money programmes and productivity improvement programmes. It is a time to develop new corporate strategies. At the beginning of this section we suggested that crisis could be predicted. Taking this a step further we can identify a number of organisational syndromes. These are, as follows:

(a)   Tightly controlled and inflexible.
(b)   Systems focus and internal orientation.
(c)   Personal style and ineffectively co-ordinated.
(d)   Paralysis through bureaucracy and lack of clear leadership.
(e)   Leaderless and constant struggle for power.

2. Management and technology

A key element in the management of turnaround is ensuring the timely and effective application of new technology. Attitudes towards new technology can generate a limited view and prevent proper usage. Misconceptions arise from failure to appreciate feedback. Positive or negative feedback controls the speed and direction of new technology because they are channels for interaction with social needs and values.

Flexible automation can allow high volumes at lower costs whilst enabling the manufacturer to produce product variations. Therefore volume and cost considerations no longer need to dominate consumer taste as in the early Ford days ('You can have any colour as long as its black'). We tend to see technological and scientific advances in isolation from each other. Instead, they should be mutually reinforcing and beneficial so as to understand that they usually only have real impact when developments converge as with telecommunications and computers. Technology has allowed us to widen the scope of information and speed up its process.

3. Information technology

The UNESCO definition of information technology stresses the links placed between technology and social and cultural patterns. The wealth of that information is relatively easy to demonstrate. Examples of how knowing something enables cost reduction through better management and greater utilisation of resources abound. Examples illustrate the social and cultural impact of technology and our increasing ability to harness technology and make it work in specific ways, for example, airline booking systems which in real time link 250 airlines worldwide, supermarket checkouts that inform stock control, thus linking input and output.

4. Micro electronics

Desk top computers are small and relatively cheap and quick, and powerful enough to perform any task that human instructions can logically define. Today, wide areas of human labour can be taken over by micro electronics. They not only take over the laborious or dangerous functions but can perform faster and better in some areas, for example computer aided design of virtually everything that needs to be designed. Specialist systems can be computerised to distil specialist knowledge and lift routine tedium from lawyers, doctors and other professionals. The onset of computers reduces the need for people between the origins of products and end users, so through a reduction in the cost of labour through automated production, greater wealth is being produced by fewer though more highly skilled people. Therefore new technology equals new wealth, equals new demand, equals new jobs, but the process is accelerating and people will need to be retrained several times throughout their normal working life in order to keep pace with it. The impact of this on mass employment needs new thinking around careers and the notion of 'a job for life'.

Issues around employment need re-thinking. Such technological advances do not necessarily mean less jobs with greater wealth for fewer people, but we need to find new ways of thinking about work and leisure. This will mean changes in our social and personal priorities and using wealth to create opportunities for recreation, education, community and public service.

In this chapter an examination has been made of some of the issues to be faced in managing technology. Doing so in crisis or turnaround situations adds to the complexity though not necessarily to the difficulty. Crisis, whilst avoided normally by the proactive manager, can concentrate mind and energy.

Exercise

What are the key issues involved in the management of turnaround? How do you view the future of work in view of the impact of technology? What measures can be taken to ensure continuity of employment?

CHAPTER 9

Small business management

Small business is often seen as distinctive. Indeed many see small business as one of the 'engines of growth' in the economy. Entrepreneurs create new businesses to exploit new business opportunities. Fast growing small firms generate employment. These views are not without difficulty. However, we can certainly say that small businesses are an important part of the economy and that managers in small businesses need many skills. In this chapter we will consider some of the issues facing managers setting up and running small businesses. We will consider the role of the entrepreneur and finally outline some of the main forms of assistance available to the small business. Whilst some of what we will say must be set within the UK legal and institutional context, we shall try to minimise this, partly for the non-UK reader, partly because the situation is changing all of the time, partly because many detailed and excellent books are available. Here we wish only to give an overview.

Key learning points

1. The role of the small business

In general small businesses perform common functions. They provide a form of competition to larger firms by being able to provide 'one-offs' which large businesses cannot accommodate. Often, they are potential seed beds as part of large corporations in the future. The intimate harmonious work environment where owners and employees are on familiar terms tends to lead to fewer industrial disputes and reduced absenteeism. In deprived areas, small businesses can re-generate employment. However, by nature, they have to be innovative and flexible in order to survive. Obviously this is a simplified overview and we can find many exceptions to these factors but identifying common features aids our understanding of the issues and problems which small businesses experience.

It is a fact that small businesses fulfil an important function in society. However, they do experience a number of operational difficulties. They often feel they get a poor deal in the grand scale of things and that governments ignore their needs and concentrate on policies to aid the large corporations whilst being insensitive to the needs of the smaller company and their importance in terms of the total economy. Problems can occur when small businesses experience growth when business practices performed previously are no longer appropriate to deal with the new changes. Growth brings with it new problems. The owner/manager can no longer expect to devote all his time to the mixed bag of issues he once did and therefore is in danger of being consumed by day to day detail. The new situation needs adapting to and more sophisticated techniques developed. What is needed is a shift in emphasis on functions, delegation and managerial expertise.

2. Management of small businesses

Planning ahead is a key issue in the survival of small businesses. Decisions tend to be made as short term strategies to overcome current problems. Therefore decisions cope with short term survival and are generally related to the sales function. However, filling order books is only one aspect; there are many others and all need a more detailed thought process. It is essential in this analysis to look at the type of customer the orders represent. If a high proportion of these are slow payers or bad debtors then it will result in a cash gap. Attention must be paid to achieving a healthy cash flow. The older the debt, the less attractive its value. Therefore the pace at which debts are cleared will affect the flow of monies circulating in the business. Another important issue is the amount of stock which is held and what that stock is doing. The balance between raw materials, work in progress and the amount of finished goods must be managed in order to control stock and prevent assets from being tied up for too long.

Growth cannot simply be related to sales volume. Growth occurs in small businesses when it can improve the quality of its earnings by increasing turnover and/or eliminating low profit areas thus increasing its liquidity in a way which does not have a decreasing effect on other areas.

3. The entrepreneur

The success and failure characterised by entrepreneurism is of great interest and fascination to us. Entrepreneurs are 'one off' exceptions to the rule; deviants. De Vries (1980) describes the entrepreneur as 'creative destructor', highly complex and creative. He conceives an idea, and implements it, going through a process of innovation, management co-ordination and risk taking. The entrepreneur needs high levels of achievement motivation, autonomy and individualism. The shape of the entrepreneur's organisation is like a spider's web with the entrepreneur at the centre. He is in control. Subordinates are often dependent in a situation which is both ambiguous and stressful. As the organisation grows powerful, interest groups enter and the strength of the entrepreneur becomes diffused. Often at this time, the survival of the organisation is in danger and separation must occur. The entrepreneur needs new challenges to divest his interest and energy into. Entrepreneurs seem capable of both vision and action. They generate new ideas and see them through to reality. They attract other people, attracting their imagination and support. But most of all they need an institutional setting that is supportive and rewarding.

4. New venture strategies

If we subscribe to the view that business units need to be recognised and given substantial autonomy, and in doing so they will become more innovative and productive, then a more action orientated approach is needed. This can be achieved by the following:

(a)   Identifying and supporting potential entrepreneurs within organisations.

(b)   Putting together teams of people with relevant skills.

(c)   Setting up companies under the umbrella of larger organisations.

(d)   Relinquishing control.

Developing the entrepreneurial spirit in organisations is vital to company development.

Exercise

In the growth of a small business what aspects need to be paid particular attention to and why? What is the role of the entrepreneur, either independently or within organisational settings?

CHAPTER 10

The wider implications organisations

In an increasingly complex business environment companies and organisations interact in a variety of ways. All of us are increasingly aware of the wider impact of decisions made by people in organisations on the wider community. Whether we are concerned with product safety, environmental pollution, consumer protection, employment policies or other matters we are concerned with aspects of the relations of organisations with society.

This chapter examines four related topics as follows:

1. Relationships between organisations and society, primarily to identify the main areas of concern and to consider the question of social responsibility.
2. The stakeholder model, considered as a model of organisational decision-making and adaptation.
3. The relationships between organisations is becoming an increasingly important aspect of managerial work.
4. The notion of 'corporatism', a model of how the state sets out to influence organisations.

Key learning points

1. The stakeholder model

Management literature stresses the separation of ownership from control of large companies and hence the need for the management group to satisfy the interests of other groups such as shareholders who may otherwise threaten the independent viability of the organisation and hence the position of the incumbent management group. In particular circumstances the survival and viability of an organisation may be threatened by the actions of such groups. Varieties of groups have interests in the success of the enterprise so for example, employees may feel the need for strike action to protect or enhance their 'stake'. Therefore, management has come to recognise the need to pursue policies towards all stakeholders in the hope of maintaining long term viability of the enterprise.

Growth of the business enterprise benefits all stakeholders – consumers, shareholders and investors, employees, government, managements and suppliers. This stakeholder orthodoxy can be regarded as having adaptive capacities as stakeholders' values and expectations change. It can be argued that these will be reflected in their changed expectations of the organisation's performance and thus affect the terms on which they will be prepared to support the enterprise. In order to pursue the objectives of survival, profitability and growth the stakeholder orthodoxy propounds that management must balance the interests of all stakeholders and seek to adapt to their changed expectation when the need arises. In practice such a view requires the acceptance of management of wider responsibilities. Inherent in this view is the meaningful concept of social responsibility; a matter of how far a company deals with its environment by incorporating external concerns into its decision-making process.

2. Organisations and society

Over the past number of years, we have seen through the media a growing awareness of organisations' moral and ethical standards. The social environment in which the organisation operates demands accountability when boundaries are broken. Examples would include pollution, dumping of nuclear waste, planning regulations, drug testing and usage, to mention but a few of many issues. Organisations must now have social responsibility; a concern for the welfare of society. Now laws exist to control safety, pollution, etc., but responsibility extends beyond this. It has obligations to shareholders, consumers and the community. Managers today have to consider their decisions and actions in relation to society at large.

If the consumer decides for some reason to withdraw its support this will affect the profitability and health of the business. Therefore a kind of social contract exists between business and society. If the public does not approve of a product it can withdraw support. So, organisations have to be aware of their public image. In order that organisations achieve their own ends, it must cater to the demands which society imposes. Many organisations are seen to be investing money towards improving the environment and providing educational opportunities through schemes such as sponsorship. This benefits the company's public image and provides constructive benefits for members of society.

Arguments against social responsibility centre around profit maximisation. Milton Friedman argues that social responsibility is not the province of corporations. He believes that responsibility should be accorded to stockholders and it is management's job to make as much money as possible for them. Money spent on social considerations erodes profit and in turn, raises prices, lowers wages and has a negative impact on society. Social responsibility for the business translates into ethical considerations for the individual. Codes of ethics are important to the business person as he takes responsibility for the organisation. Individuals are required to make statements and comments which reflect the company and its policies. The individual has to find a balance between his views and beliefs whilst maintaining the interests of his company.

Difficult moral and ethical decisions have to be made by managers at certain times. Imagine a company which is about to make a number of its workforce redundant. A difficult decision has to be made. The decision will hinge on the ethical principles of the organisation and on the values and beliefs of the individuals involved in making that decision.

3. Corporatism

Corporatism refers to the way in which governments take an increasingly directive role in relation to industry directly through mechanisms such as central planning and government, management and union negotiations and discussions, and indirectly, through institutions such as the Manpower Services Commission in Britain. Whilst there is a great diversity worldwide, there are some trends worth noting. Governments take a role in macro-economic policy thus affecting competitiveness, productivity and providing support for strategically important industries. The extent and form of government ownership varies across the world. Recently, governments have established joint ventures in various business areas with foreign multi-nationals. These create new problems and opportunities for management. The corporatist tendency includes attempts by government to in-corporate managers and trade unions into the institutional framework by means of de-politicising these problems, en-couraging co-operation, commitment and national stability and success.

Exercise

Is social responsibility a choice or a necessity for organisations? Use examples from your own experience or issues you are familiar with to illustrate your arguments.

CHAPTER 11

Case study review

This section summarises the learning points for the cases presented in the text, *Management: Principles and Policy*, ICSA Publishing Limited, 1988 by Colin Carnall and Susan Maxwell.

Managerial skills for managing change

Example: EDP case

Summary of key learning points

- The EDP case illustrates the problems associated with managing change.
- People perceive, experience and interpret problems depending upon how they are affected by change. Consequently change can become very threatening and be resisted.
- When change causes a series of problems we often lose sight of the core issues and become saturated by data. This limits our thinking and prohibits us taking a 'helicopter' view of events.
- The EDP case highlights how these problems build up into pressure points. Those involved become stressed and problem-solving is blocked. No-one is able to take a broad perspective as fear of failure is too great and risk taking is low.

- Such blocks inhibit creative thinking, therefore these blocks need to be identified and worked through in order to release creativity and find solutions.
- Change, if viewed as problematic, can have a negative effect on self-esteem and psychological well-being. Those orchestrating change need to recognise their responsibility in helping subordinates through the process and offer practical support.
- Support can be provided by keeping staff well informed, empathising with their problems, providing support and encouragement to learn from change, teaching new skills and providing appropriate training.
- Handling corporate politics is also part of change. We need to recognise where political power bases exist, both formally and informally. Knowledge and use of networks are key factors in influencing change-makers.
- To manage change effectively we need to reduce resistance from subordinates. In doing this we make it easier and more comfortable to implement change from above.

Small business management

Example: Grant Electronics case

Summary of key learning points

- Grant Electronics illustrates the problems small businesses experience when growth takes place.
- The case also illustrates an example of the independent entrepreneur. He 'goes it alone' as a means of expressing himself.
- Typical of such entrepreneurs, John Grant is the central point of control within the organisation and whilst the company was small enough, he could exercise this effectively.
- As the business grows and expands, other expertise is required. A professional management approach is increasingly required.
- As the size and complexity of the business develops it

will no longer afford the autonomy which the entrepreneur needs. Therefore he will become frustrated and uneasy. The organisational culture is no longer supportive or rewarding. In these circumstances the entrepreneur will suffer role deterioration.

- Large corporations often do not provide a culture conducive to the entrepreneurial spirit. However, large organisations need innovators and must find ways to attract their talents. The 'model' entrepreneur with values and education which are in harmony with corporate structures could harness his talents towards organisational goals.

Conditions for effective change

Example: A financial institution case

Summary of key learning points

- The financial institution case illustrates the need for change and how that can be accomplished effectively.
- The culture operating within the organisation was not appropriate for a task orientated function.
- Bureaucratic structures work well in stable environments where roles are clearly defined and a rigid hierarchy operates to deal with decision making.
- Such a system was obstructing the objectives of a task orientated function.
- The system needed to be decentralised and organised into small, task orientated teams headed by those with the relevant expertise.
- More autonomy was needed to cope with the varying task demands so groups could achieve their goals.
- The culture of an organisation is dependent upon what needs it must fulfil, and the rate at which change affects it.
- Power cultures fit organisations which need tight control. These are typically characterised in small, growing

companies where success is dependent upon the leader's strength and personality.

- As the external environment changes, organisations need to change too. In order to do this effectively, they must reduce their weaknessness and build upon their strengths. The financial institution case study shows how change can be effective by diagnosing the problem, innovating and involving the participants.

Managerial accountability

Example: Role of the supervisor in a process plant company case

Summary of key learning points

- The role of the supervisor case illustrates the issues of managerial accountability and responsibility within the roles of supervisor and subordinates in a specific job.
- Healthy working relationships between departments within organisations are important in getting tasks done.
- Team work is crucial to promote confidence and build self-esteem. Therefore good working practices are the responsibility of bosses and peers.
- In complex operations which also involve geographical distance, control and communications can become difficult. These need to be recognised and maintained by liaising with other departments.
- Supervisors need support and backing from management and appropriate styles need to be developed in order to manage effectively.
- Managers are constrained by internal and external factors. External may mean health and safety regulations, Trade Union practices, location. Internal may mean organisational policy, attitudes, procedures.
- Authority gives the right to exercise power. This can be functional (helpful, positive) or dysfunctional (restrictive, negative) to those working under it. Managers have

choices and responsibilities to those who work for them
and with them.

Management work and managerial performance

Example: ABF Ltd case

Summary of key learning points

- ABF Ltd is an example of an organisation which has
  become ineffective and of how this affects performance.
- The management style of the managing director is auto-
  cractic. This, in turn, has led to poor delegation which in
  turn has stifled initiative.
- Communication is poor. Personnel are unaware of what
  is happening in the company and have become sus-
  picious and defensive.
- Management style is insular and inward looking. 'Con-
  forming' is the watch-word. Therefore, commitment is
  low. Change is something that is feared and threatening.
- Objectives have not been modified to fit new circumstances and the changing external environment.
- Attitudes are closed. Performance is not discussed openly and constructively. Criticism is seen as negative,
  therefore difficult situations are avoided, and, worse
  still they are seen as emotional, not rational.
- As a consequence of this issues are avoided and possible
  solutions never sought.
- For organisations to be effective they need to be adaptable to changing situations, from the external, e.g. the
  market, competition, etc., and the internal, e.g. style of
  leadership and management.
- Performance needs to be monitored and discussed openly in order that goals and objectives are clearly articulated. Thus effectiveness can be achieved and both
  organisational and individual needs will be met and
  excellence achieved.

Managerial motivation and development

Example: CAC Consultants case

Summary of key learning points

- The CAC Consultants case illustrates the role of management development within organisations and the resistance this may cause.
- It also illustrates the divergence of opinion around the topic of career development – those who adopted a *laissez faire* attitude (recruitment) to career development and those who saw it as a planned, integral part of the organisation (developmental).
- The main issue, that of career development, got lost as each interest group pushed their own opinions forward. Emotions were seen as threatening and resulted in defensive behaviour.
- Management development needs to be integrated within company policy. Goals need to be agreed as to where the organisation is going and what resources it needs to accomplish this. It is part of managerial effectiveness through developing competency within managers.
- Management development needs to be a positive experience. Therefore it must involve:
    1. Identifying what and who are needed for the organisation to develop.
    2. Confirming through training and development programmes which are appropriate both for the organisation's and the individual's needs.
    3. Having the commitment of all parties involved.
- Management development programmes require flexibility to accommodate self development and provide a total learning process for those on it to learn and benefit from successes and failures.
- CAC Consultants need to find ways of providing both commitment and motivation for the organisation to develop as a whole. All interest groups could have their

needs met through a programme designed around management and career development issues.

The wider implications of organisations

Example: Three Mile Island case

Summary of key learning points

- Three Mile Island represents a highly complex situation. It is about social responsibility because it not only affects the organisation itself but also a wider society. Therefore how it operates will be scrutinised by the public as it directly affects the public.
- Poor communication lead to misunderstanding by those directly involved in dealing with the crisis. This was further compounded by inadequate training procedures which meant vital information was ignored.
- Unrealistic attitudes had been fostered by an erroneous belief that a crisis could not happen despite the existence of evidence to the contrary at another plant.
- Several organisations were involved (the operator, the contractors, the Nuclear Regulatory Commission) which led to a divergence of interest.
- Therefore Three Mile Island not only provides us with an example of how organisations have a wider impact on society, but also illustrates the complex nature of problems and how we try to solve them.

Case study analysis

PART TWO

Case study analysis

CHAPTER 12

The case study method

Case study method is widely used in management education. Case studies provide students with opportunities to think for themselves through the presentation of managerial and organisational situations and facts. A case study will provide background information to a particular issue and relate a set of events and administrative problems that confront either an individual within an organisation or the organisation itself. From the information presented, the student must then analyse the situation, identify problems, make decisions and draw conclusions. As case studies are based on actual situations and experiences, they provide a rich source of theorectical and practical learning. To maximise the full potential of case study method, students should be encouraged, whenever possible, to discuss the case amongst themselves or in small groups, thus exchanging ideas and enriching the breadth of learning.

The aims of the case study method are as follows:

1. To achieve knowledge.
2. To understand techniques and acquire the skill to use techniques.
3. To be able to analyse complex and unstructured problems.
4. To synthesise knowledge and plan for action.
5. To distinguish between hopes and beliefs against facts and actualities.
6. To understand the issues of business and institutions, both moral and ethical.

7.   To develop judgement and be able to foresee outcomes and consequences both from long term and short term perspectives.
8.   To develop self criticism and consider the opinions of others.
9.   To crystalise succinctly the major facts and objectives and produce these in a clear concise manner.

How to prepare for a case study

Below is an example of a case study. This particular case 'Peter Morrow – A case study in career development' relates to the problems and issues an individual is having at a specific point in his career. Read the case several times. This may sound obvious but a thorough knowledge of its contents is essential prior to answering the questions.

Peter Morrow – a case study in career development

Peter Morrow left university aged 21 with a second class honours degree in Maths. and Science. Like many graduates he had no clear career ideas about his future. At university he had been good within his subject area and had also enjoyed a wide variety of sports and leisure activities, though he had not excelled in any of these. His friends found him quiet but likeable.

After seeking advice from the university's careers centre and the 'milk round' he thought that he would like a career in finance or banking but was not entirely clear why he felt this way. He liked the impression of style and power he felt was associated with this kind of work. Several applications to banks and other financial institutions brought no success and Peter was both disappointed and puzzled by this lack of progress. Within a relatively short period of time, Peter was able to secure a position as a trainee accountant in a small subsidiary, Hills Ltd, of a large engineering company, AB Group (see Fig. 12.1). Although there was no formalised training scheme, the company did encourage day release to study for a relevant professional qualification. Peter was delighted.

Hills Ltd is managed by a managing director with financial director, works manager and sales managers. The managing

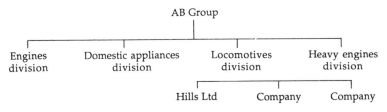

Fig. 12.1 Organisation chart of AB Group.

director was a member of the locomotive division, but not of the AB Group board. Personnel was a group function along with business development, marketing and research and development. The structure of the organisation was such that each subsidiary was run as a virtually autonomous unit; so long as each unit continued to be profitable, little intervention was made by the parent company.

Peter was now faced with the choice of which professional qualification to study for. The local poly-technic offered a wide range of suitable courses, all of which seemed likely to fit his career needs. It seemed sensible to him to ask around the company and find out which qualifications his colleagues possessed. His immediate superior was a certified accountant and though this was a well recognised qualification, Peter remembered friends telling him it was limited. Being a small company, the financial director also had the role of company secretary. During a conversation with the financial director, Peter learned that he was a chartered secretary. Knowing little about this, Peter enquired further and was told that this qualification offered both accountancy and administrative skills. The financial director explained that his job required these skills. It seemed obvious to Peter that this man had been successful, so he decided that it would be a good idea to study for CIS.

Over the next five years Peter stayed with the company. He gained his CIS qualification, a wife, a son and had been promoted through to company accountant. Over this period he developed accountancy skills and a thorough understanding of accounting systems controls and also got to know the business well. The financial director was by now approaching retirement and during the past year Peter had become increasingly responsible for the company's financial functions. Over the past 18 months the parent company had been radically reorganised and many key positions changed. Head office was taking tighter control and increasing its demands for cash generation and cost control. The financial director found these changes difficult to cope with and consequently passed more responsibility to Peter. He responded well to these challenges and generally the parent company seemed happy with his progress. However, Peter was having difficulty passing decisions through the financial director and was constantly having to by-pass him and deal directly with the divisionary board to get decisions. The financial director felt threatened and Peter found the situation stressful.

Struggling with two jobs, Peter was having to work long hours and this was causing pressure at home. His wife felt isolated and lonely and his son was constantly crying. Peter found this both confusing and frustrating. The financial director decided to take early retirement and there was much speculation about his replacement. Peter believed he stood a good chance of getting the job. After all, he had virtually been doing the job for 3 years, he had built good relations between himself and the parent company, and he believed he had coped well with a difficult situation. Although he recognised he was a little young for such a position, he believed his experience would over-ride this.

The company appointed a 34 year old chartered accountant recruited from outside the organisation for the post.

Feeling disappointed and unfairly treated, Peter decided it was time for a career move and began to look for another job. He contacted several employment agencies and scanned accounting journals and newspapers such as the Daily Telegraph and the Financial Times. Although he had a great deal of experience within one organisation it was clear to him when writing his C.V. that his lack of employment experience may be a problem. He also realised that he had not attended courses and conferences which could support his experience. In retrospect Peter realised this was unfortunate but he had never had time for such things. Several interviews brought no job offers and after three months he began to become concerned and not a little anxious about the situation. He spent much time trying to find an explanation but each time he could not find a solution. During his fourth month Peter was offered and accepted the job as group accountant with a young, rapidly expanding group of companies with diverse business interests. The group comprised a holding company and some two dozen subsidiary companies in building, project management, electrical contracting and leisure activities. The opportunity to gain a wide breadth of experience was appealing and in such a rapidly growing organisation there appeared to be many avenues to expand his career. The organisation had some doubts in offering Peter the job but his enthusiasm and previous experience convinced them.

This new job meant that Peter was based at head office and he felt this would enable him to build good relations with senior personnel and influence company policy more directly. The workload was heavy and principally mundane but it was also interesting and offered variety. Running the management accounting system and producing year end figures was mundane and time-consuming (at the year end!). Dealing with the varying accounting needs of the very diverse businesses within the group provided variety and challenge. Establishing loyalty was something of a problem. Each company believed their problems most urgent and so the demands they made were often unreasonable. This was compounded by the role 'head office man' which was treated with some suspicion and caution by managers in the various companies.

After three years in this role Peter began to feel anxious about his career. He had learned much about the problems of each company and although he recognised the value of this, he was sensitive to the fact that his financial expertise had grown little. There was also a growing awareness that he reported directly to the financial director who was a man in his mid-forties and realistically this was the only career avenue available to progress to. Peter knew there was little chance of this position becoming vacant and if it did, he doubted whether he had the financial expertise it demanded. On the other hand, the company was pleased with Peter's work. He had tightened up the company's financial systems and they had rewarded him with a succession of salary increases and given him a quality company car.

Around this time there were several disagreements amongst the directors and as a result of this, a de-merger was planned. This put Peter in a commanding position; both factions needed his skills. Finally, he chose to move with the newly found property division. Though he had least expertise here he was aware of its potential growth and liked the idea of working with a dynamic group of people. Consequently Peter was promoted to financial controller, given a higher salary, improved fringe benefits and a prestigous car. Peter enjoyed working with creative dynamic people to begin with but became rapidly uncomfortable with their constantly changing ideas and disregard for financial strategies. The situation become one of constant conflict and Peter was finding the stress impossible. Added to his, his wife and growing family were becoming increasingly dissatisfied with the quality of their lives. At lunch one day with business acquaintances, Peter discussed his problems and the conversation resulted in him being offered a position with another organisation. Their needs are for financial streamlining and to prepare them for future expansion. Peter is considering this offer.

Exercise

1.   What are Peter's strengths and weaknesses?
2.   Can you suggest how Peter may have improved his career history?
3.   Consider the options Peter has open to him now. What decision do you think he should make?

Peter Morrow's self-assessment

Since I began working I have become very ambitious. My major aim is to be successful. Although I am aware that my career up to now has been a reasonable success, I have a good salary, company car and other benefits, I still feel that I have not achieved my full potential. Because of this, I feel frustrated with my career and generally dissatisfied with life.

I enjoy the type of work I do and find it interesting and stimulating. Therefore, I am happy with my actual job choice. I also believe I am competent and have valuable skills which others recognise. New challenges are important to me as I see them as a way of proving myself to my superiors. Independence is important to me too. I like to be free to make decisions and follow them through. I am well disciplined and feel a strong sense of responsibility in my work. I like to know all the facts before I make decisions and often feel other people take too many risks. I have respect for those who are successful and feel I can learn a lot from them.

The most difficult thing I find to cope with is working with other people. It is much easier for me to work alone. Working in teams is frustrating and time consuming and I feel the time used is often wasted as everyone is only interested in expressing their particular point of view and therefore little is ever achieved. Socialising with colleagues is also an area which is difficult for me. Because I am quiet and introverted, this is often seen to be anti-social, though this is not my intention. I enjoy working and frequently take work home with me at evenings or weekends. This is necessary as I always have a lot of work in progress. Generally my wife and family accept this, though there are times when it causes pressure. However, on the whole, my family are supportive and realise how important it is for my career. I have gained significant expertise in my career area but realise my career could level off at this stage. As I want career growth to continue I must make efforts towards this but I find it difficult under the circumstances.

1.   Begin by trying to identify problems. What issues is Peter Morrow confronting? On the surface it may appear a simple question of career choice but, if we examine the case in depth, we discover several issues have amalgamated into 'the problem'. So, list any points which seem relevant at this juncture.

2.   Look for ambiguities and inconsistencies. Try to identify weaknesses in the case where there is scant information. Compare Peter's career history with his self-assessment and spot points which conflict. Identify his strengths and weaknesses both as an individual and within the context of his career history.

3.   Clarify the problem – ask yourself, 'What is being asked? Sometimes issues are clearly stated, other times they may be obscure. In case studies real problems are often enmeshed in several other issues. Relevant facts and information need to be drawn out now in order that you gain a clear perception of the problem. Discussion with other students is particularly helpful at this point. The

exchange of ideas and an opportunity to express varied opinions will help to clarify issues and identify different perceptions of the problems.

4.   Once the problems have been identified, they must be broken down into priorities. Which issues are central and what are the key facts? What are the sub-issues that bear consideration to the major problem? There may be several solutions to the problem and a choice will have to be made based on the information extrapolated from the case. It is clear that Peter Morrow has more than one alternative open to him. Identify these and examine their implications. What is realistic under the circumstances, what are the risks inherent in each alternative, are they worth taking? Consider the various options – sift through the information and relate it to the alternatives.

5.   You should now have reached the point where you can make a decision on a course of action. Produce an outline plan which covers the steps you have taken in formulating your analysis. Identify weaknesses and strengths *within* the plan. Draw out both the opportunities and limitations of your decision.

6.   Remember, there is no 'right answer' in most case studies, but a selection of possible solutions. Some will be sounder than others. Selecting the most appropriate course of action will result from an examination of factors such as time, expectations, conditions, etc.

Presentation of solution

This must describe a realistic and workable solution and illustrate the analysis of the problems. For example, you may decide that Peter needs to improve his level of qualifications in order to broaden his career opportunities. Consider a realistic approach to this, bearing in mind his financial and marital commitments. What problems would he have to address and do you think from the information you have about Peter that he would be prepared to reduce his living standards, albeit for a relatively short period, and take the risk of creating a gap in his career? How would his wife and family respond to this and what kinds of changes would it make to their out-of-work lives? Not only do you need to draw from the information within the case, but also relate this to experiences you may have come across either yourself, at work or with friends and relations, thus using both a theoretical framework and practical application in order to draw your conclusions.

Solutions need to be consistent with the facts and assumptions in the case. Presentation is individualistic. However, you will find it useful to consider the following points in your presentations as a means of reviewing your work:

1.   State the problem(s) clearly and concisely.
2.   Identify the factors involved in the problem(s).
3.   Explain why they are problems.
4.   Review possible alternatives to the problem(s) and their implications.
5.   Conclusions must be based on your analysis and related to the case.

A final point

As the authors mentioned earlier, discussion is an integral part of case study analysis, contributing through the process of questioning helps students to test out facts. Constructive comment and criticism by students and tutors will lead to a more thought-provoking and broader analysis of the issues.

Summary of key learning points

- Motivation is a key aspect of management development.
- Career development is the planning each individual needs to do in order to give careers direction.
- Management development is part of company policy and provides a structure through which the individual can express his career needs.
- Responsibility for career is that of both the individual – expressing and accomplishing his needs and the organisation – providing the opportunity for this to happen and, in doing this, achieving the organisation's goals and objectives.
- People need to be motivated in order to work to their maximum potential. In order to create motivation we have to develop an awareness of both the organisation's

needs and the needs of that individual within the organisation.

- Peter Morrow was highly 'achievement' orientated but he lacked both career planning and management development. To maximise his full potential he needed to develop a career goal and seek out organisations which would provide him with the necessary training and development to realise his career goal.

CHAPTER 13

Planning for implementation – introducing 'right first time'

You are the general manager of an organisation which has achieved rapid growth in the last six years. The number of employees has increased by 150% over that period, whilst income has increased by 220% over the same period. It now employs 6,000 people organised into eight functional departments, including a personnel, organisation and methods and finance department. You were appointed from outside to replace the previous general manager who retired two years ago. The growth programme is complete and you expect the organisation to remain at its present size for the next five years.

Since taking over your appointment you have encountered many examples of administrative systems and procedures which seem inefficient. For example, the reward system for managers comprised a complex framework of grades and pay levels, merit awards, special allowances and other payments. A study undertaken at your instructions demonstrated that the majority of your managers did not understand the reward system and that it was costly to administer. In consequence you undertook a detailed review of the system, with full participation of the managers concerned, which led to a significantly rationalised system of managerial rewards. Many other examples had come to your attention in your first year in the organisation. A year ago you instituted a programme which you named the 'Right First Time' programme. The aim of this programme was to improve the quality of administrative systems and procedures throughout the organisation. You established the principles of the programme in an announcement to all employees. An example announcement is:

All work is carried out for a customer or client. In some cases the customer/client is outside the organisation. In other situations the customer/client is the individual or department affected by the work, perhaps taking over what has been done to complete a subsequent stage. Having achieved dramatic growth over recent years we must now ensure that our systems and procedures are put into good order. We must strive to achieve 'Right First Time'. To do so will require the full participation of people at all levels in the organisation and also a major programme of training and education. All this will be set in train in the coming months. I ask for your help and commitment in making this programme a success.

Since then a working party comprising the eight departmental heads has been formed to plan a quality improvement programme and a related training programme focusing upon problem-solving techniques, quality monitoring techniques, meeting skills and participation skills. Mixed groups of managers, supervisors and employees (30 on each course) attend a one-week course at a hotel. Over a period of two years all employees will participate in this training programme. Subsequently, 'Right First Time' meetings will be held in departments to identify and then resolve problems within the department. Early indications are that this programme is generating significant enthusiasm, and that a number of administrative problems are being overcome rapidly.

You are required to respond to the following questions:

1. Describe the role of the general manager in this programme of change and discuss its importance.
2. Outline in broad terms how you might set about evaluating the effectiveness of the 'Right First Time' programme.
3. Outline the measures you might adopt to follow-up and exploit the early success of the programme.

This question may be dealt with from the perspective of either a private sector organisation (for eample a commercial organisation or the administrative part of a manufacturing company) or a public sector organisation. State the type of organisation you are considering. Each part of the question carries equal marks.

ICSA, December 1985

Identify the problem

Here is a success story. The organisation has achieved rapid growth over a six year period. The number of employees has grown 150% over the period whilst income has increased 220% over the same period. We are not told anything about the prevailing rates of inflation over the period nor whether or not 150% increase in staffing means more or less than 150% increase in staff costs (this depends upon issues such as the extent of shift working, over-time working, incentive pay systems and the staff profile). Nevertheless it seems not unreasonable to suppose that given inflation, the 220% increase in turnover is not particularly impressive.

The organisation is of medium size, and is organised functionally. The present general manager took post two years ago to replace a retiring general manager who had overseen the first four of a six year period of growth. Despite the growth record, perhaps because of the growth and its attendant pressures, there is plenty of evidence of problems. Administrative systems and procedures are complex and unwieldy. The general manager has already seen through a rationalisation programme for the managerial reward systems. It is clear that many similar opportunities for improvement exist. The general manager therefore faces the problem of how to galvanise the organisation into action. Having been successful, many people might feel that changes to administrative systems and procedures are not needed. The general manager needs to generate support and commitment to an action programme aimed at identifying and implementing improvements. To this end he has instituted a 'Right First Time' programme. The slogan is simple and powerful. The announcement of the programme identifies the importance of the customer or client. It refers to the growth of recent years, but goes on to say that the organisation must now put its systems and procedures into good order.

This will involve full participation. Training programmes have been instituted and significant activity is underway. There seems to have been significant enthusiasm and good, initial, results. The problem then is that under the pressures created by growth in activity, systems have not been adapted to meet the new circumstances. It is likely that as new situations arose new procedures and systems were added. Thus systems have become complex and fragmented. So much so that staff no longer fully understand the systems as a whole, what they are intended to achieve, nor all of the rules and procedures which apply.

Look for ambiguities or weaknesses

The description of the organisation provided suggests complex administrative problems. Moreover, we are told that the managerial reward system is complex and that the majority of managers do not understand it. A reasonable assumption to make is that many people, at all levels in the organisation, experience considerable frustration with these various problems. The change programme has started off with early success. The general manager must sustain momentum and enthusiasm. This will not be easy because the frustrations of 'fire-fighting', dealing with today's problems, can often absorb all the energy people have. Change also creates its own doubts, and will be stressful. Thus the early enthusiasm can easily be dissipated.

Clarify the problem

Thus the problem is that of sustaining the programme of change, building on early success, monitoring results, providing feedback. The role of the general manager is that of generating wide understanding of the crucial importance of the change programme. The general manager needs to agree a programme of change, with clear objectives and targets. These must be measurable. Individual managers must be identified and made accountable. Evaluation of the effectiveness of the programme can focus upon individual, departmental and organisational factors, including attitudes and morale, efficiency, wastage, complaints and so on.

Key issues

These include leadership, management style, the pace and momentum of change, how to monitor change and the crucial importance of feedback.

Identify a plan

In dealing with a case study question in the examination course members should respond to the questions posed. Usually some sort of outline plan will be required. The main issues to be addressed and related problems can be identified by working through the implementation exercise set out in the next section.

Exercise

The following checklists identify a range of problems and solutions available to students interested to develop viable plans for change. Case studies will always require students to identify plans for change. Students who familiarise themselves with the key items set out below will have a structured way of setting out a case study response dealing with issues to be addressed when plans are to be developed and implemented.

The two checklists in the exercise each deal with five areas. For each area there are potential problems dealt with by the checklist. These problems and *some* possible solutions are set out below.

Checklist 1: Readiness for change

Company 'track record' of changes

Potential problems:
1. Have past changes met with resistance?
2. Were past changes poorly understood?
3. Are employees too cautious?
4. Did recently introduced changes have limited or little success?

Solutions:
1. Keep everyone informed by making information available, explaining plans clearly, allowing access to management for questions and clarification.
2. Ensure that change is sold realistically by making a practical case for change, explain change in terms which the employee will see as relevant and acceptable, show

how change fits business needs and plans, spend time and effort on presentations.

3.   Prepare carefully by making a full organisational diagnosis, spending time with people and groups, building trust, understanding and support.

4.   Involve people by getting feedback on proposals, getting people to fill out the checklists, discussing the data from these checklists.

5.   Start small and successful piloting with a receptive group of employees, piloting in departments with a successful track record, implement changes in clear phases.

6.   Plan for success by starting with things that can give a quick and positive payoff, publicise early success, provide positive feedback to those involved in success.

Expectations of change

Potential problems:
- Do different people hold different ideas about the change?
- Do people know what to expect?
- Are objectives clearly defined?

Solutions:
- Clarify benefits of changes by emphasising benefits to those involved, to the company.
- Minimise surprises by specifying all assumptions about the change, focus on outcomes, identify potential problems.
- Communicate plans by being specific in *terms* familiar to the different groups of employees, communicate periodically and through various media, ask for feedback, do not suppress negative views but listen to them carefully and deal with them openly.

Who 'owns' the problem or the idea for change?

Potential problems:
- Are the procedures, systems, departments, products, services involved seen to be a problem?

- Was the change planned or introduced by top management or staff departments?
- Is the change viewed as a matter of procedure?

Solutions:

- Specify plans in terms people understand, ensure that employees' problems are addressed explicitly as part of the change, arrange for visible outcomes.
- Clarify employees' views by exploring their concerns about the changes and examining impact on the day to day routines.
- Present a clear case by specifying who wants change and why, explain longer term advantages, identify common benefits, present potential problems clearly, listen to problems.

Top management support

Potential problems:

- Do top management support the change?
- Will top management provide resources?
- Is the management performance appraisal process an obstacle to change?

Solutions:

- Build a power base by becoming the expert in the problems involved, understand top management concerns, develop informal and formal support, develop a strong and polished presentation in top management language.
- Develop clear objectives and plans by establishing a clear timetable, set up review processes to be supportive, bring in top management and middle management to the review process, focus meetings on specific outcomes, and specific problems.

Acceptability of change

Potential problems:

- Does the planned change fit other plans?
- Is there a clear sense of direction?

- Does the proposed change place greater demands on people?
- Does the change involve new technology, products/ services, expertise?

Solutions:

- Identify relevance of change to plans by reviewing plans specifying how change fits, incorporate changes into on-going developments, if possible, frame changes in terms of the organisation's style.
- Clarify plans for change by communicating simply and openly.
- Implement with flexible or adaptable people, people familiar with some or all of the change, in a part of the business where there are strong supporters for change, recognise why people support change (career, rewards, company politics).
- Do not oversell change by being clear about conflicts with present practices, encourage discussion of these conflicts.

Checklist 2: Implementation

Clarifying plans

Potential problems:

1. Does the plan identify clear phases and deadlines?
2. Is the timetable realistic?
3. Is responsibility for change clear?

Solutions:

- Assign one person to be accountable for change.
- Define goals carefully by checking feasibility with people involved, experts, other companies, using measurable goals where possible but always looking at broader goals and outcomes.
- Define specific goals by defining small, clear steps, identifying and publicising critical milestones, assign firm deadlines.
- Translate plans to action by publishing plans, build in rewards for performance, give regular feedback.

Integrating new practices and procedures

Potential problems:
- On how wide a scale will the change be introduced?
- Is the speed of implementation too fast?
- Are people involved supportive, informed, prepared?

Solutions:
- Plan the rate of change carefully by piloting to learn from experience, implementing for success, small steps and specific milestones, allow *more* time.
- Enlist firm support, ensure that new procedures, products, services are well understood.

Providing training and support

Potential problems:
- Are we providing specific training?
- Is the training flexible and geared to people's needs?
- Are we targeting the right people for training/education?

Solutions:
- Clarify objectives of training, use existing skills and knowledge, depend on people as part of implementation, use suggestions as part of the training.
- Allow people to learn at their own pace, provide opportunities for 'hands on' experience, make training relevant to the job, have line managers 'project manage' training.
- Use different learning approaches, respect and use people's experience, allow people to solve problems and utilise their solutions.
- Incorporate feedback into training programme.

'Ownership' and commitment

Potential problems:
- Does the change impose controls on people?
- Does the change reduce managers' (or other) discretion, initiative?
- Are people affected being consulted?
- Are there incentives, benefits?

Solutions:
- Plan change to bring benefits by using it to increase personal control over the job (and accountability), enhance people's jobs and status, ensure quick, visible benefits, provide incentives for people to go for change.
- Involve people by asking for suggestions, specify milestones and ask for feedback, publicise ways in which suggestions and feedback are utilised.

Providing feedback

Potential problems:
- Do visible benefits occur only over the long term (one year)?
- Are benefits visible to top management?
- Is the impact on cost, productivity, resource utilisation, market share, etc., well documented?
- Are benefits clear and direct for the people involved?

Solutions:
- Make sure that results are well documented, accessible, quickly available, positively described, relevant, achievement of 'milestones' recognised.
- Arrange wide recognition of success of people involved throughout the organisation, specify how the change has helped the organisation achieve its goals.

CHAPTER 14

Managing creative staff – a case study

The manager of the Research and Development Department in an organisation has been treating staff in a belligerent manner. Never praised for good work, the staff are frequently reprimanded for minor errors of delays, in the presence of colleagues. Moreover, staff often feel that they are blamed unfairly. A complaint about this manager's behaviour was lodged with the manager who has overall responsibility for the department and to whom the research and development manager reports.

This manager was less concerned about the complaints of the staff than with supporting the research and development manager, whom he valued highly as someone who could ensure that targets were met. His only action was to tell the research and development manager which employees had complained. In an effort to discourage and prevent future complaints the manager scrutinized the work of those employees closely. When mistakes were made, no matter how insignificant, he would criticize, arrange for transfers to less challenging work and, in one case, reduced the merit rating of a project leader.

You are the general manager of the organisation. The personnel manager has brought this situation to your attention, informally. Your impression is that the performance of the Research and Development Department has been quite satisfactory recently. However, you know that a major effort will be required of the department in the coming year on an important, large-scale development programme.

1.   What action will you take in this situation? Give reasons.

2.   What are the likely longer term implications of your proposed actions?

Each part of the question carries equal weighting.

ICSA, December 1984

Identify the problem

In this case the research and development manager has been treating staff in an agressive manner, often seen as unfair by the staff. So much so that one member of the staff has lodged a complaint. It is reasonable to suppose that the fact that a formal complaint has been lodged indicates that feelings are running very strongly. However, please note that the case study gives no basis for explaining *why* the manager has acted in the way described.

The manager with whom the complaint has been lodged seems most concerned to support the research and development manager. We are told that he values this manager as someone who could ensure that targets are met. His response is to deal with the staff in an aggressive manner which seems likely to make the problems worse.

On the face of it, the problem is that you, the general manager, are faced with a group of key staff who feel unfairly treated to the point that one complains. Rather than follow some kind of complaints procedure the manager responsible seems to reinforce the unfair behaviour. It seems unlikely that the staff concerned will feel that justice has been done and been seen to be done.

Look for ambiguities and inconsistencies

Firstly we do not know why the research and development manager and his manager are acting in the way described. Moreover we are told that the Research and Development Department has been performing quite satisfactorily recently. Also, the research and development manager is seen as someone who could ensure that targets are met. The implication of these points is that he is an effective manager. This implies that we must look for some change in the situation to explain the behaviour.

Clarify the problem

You are the general manager. This situation has been brought to your attention by the personnel manager, on an informal basis. You are concerned about it because you know that a major effort will be expected of the Research and Development Department in the coming year. On the face of it something is wrong. This must lead you to wonder about whether or not the satisfactory performance will be undermined. This would represent a problem because it seems reasonable to suppose that you are seeking an above average performance next year. So, on the one hand you have two managers whose performance has, so far, been good. On the other hand they appear to have acted unreasonably to their staff. This is problem enough in itself, but it is all the more important because of the demands you will be making on these staff. You are therefore concerned with the linked issues of fair and reasonable treatment for staff, motivation and management style.

Key issues

Here there are two key issues. One relates to an appropriate leadership style for research and development. Relevant factors in the selection of an appropriate leadership style include those set out in the following list:
- How clearly are organisational goals defined?
- How thoroughly have goals been communicated to subordinates?
- How adequate are formal communication channels? Are both upward and downward channels provided for?
- Does the company philosophy support the predominant use of:
  (a) Fear.
  (b) Threats.
  (c) Punishment.
  (d) Rewards.
  (e) Involvement.
- How wide is the normal span of supervision and control?
- What are the leader's inclinations in terms of communicating to, listening to, and empathising with subordinates?

- What are the leader's attitudes toward involvement in decision making?
- What degree of confidence and trust does he have in the abilities and knowledge of his subordinates?
- How knowledgeable is the leader concerning decisions that are necessary and tasks that must be performed?
- How important to the leader is the development of analytical skills and self-control abilities in the subordinates?
- To what degree do subordinates accept the goals of the company, and how loyal are they to these goals?
- Do the subordinates have a relatively high need for independence?
- Are subordinates willing to assume responsibility for decision making and self-control?
- How much personal satisfaction do workers derive from the performance of their jobs?
- Are subordinates well trained, knowledgeable, and experienced at their work?
- Have subordinates shared in decision making and control processes previously?
- Are subordinates' personal goals and objectives compatible with those of the organisation?
- Do subordinates have mutually positive respect for each other?
- How much room for error is there in the task to be accomplished?
- How much time is available for making decisions and completing tasks?
- How important are new ideas and innovations to the successful task completion?

Research and development departments tend to be fluid, creative organisations in which a participative and not an autocratic style will be most appropriate. How then can we work to change the leadership style in use. Here it is a combination of counselling, management appraisal and review and manager development. The general manager needs to raise his concerns with the managers involved. It is crucial that this be carried out in a constructive way. The concern must be to ensure the continued effectiveness of research and development.

The second key issue is to develop a more appropriate ap-proach to disciplinary action. This would form part of the skills development which might be identified not only for these two, but for all management. It seems likely that these managers do not know how to provide feedback which is critical, in a construc-tive way. This is an important skill. The main principles to be followed are:

- At an early stage, the employee and manager discuss the organisation's goals and objectives. At this time the job description is discussed, and the two agree on the content of the job and the relative importance of the major duties. Together, they determine what the em-ployee is to be held accountable for.

- The employee, after some time for consideration, deter-mines performance targets for each responsibility in a specified time period.

- The employee and his manager meet to review and finalise the standards the employee has set. The targets may be modified or revised if necessary.

- Checkpoints are established for the evaluation of pro-gress. Ways of measuring performance are specified, and the employee monitors his performance regularly.

- At predetermined time intervals, the employee and his manager meet to discuss performance progress, to deter-mine corrections needed, and to modify future standards where changes are called for.

If such a progress has been established the feedback between manager and scientist can be much more constructively carried out because both are used to the process of review and feedback. Carrying it through on a regular basis leads to a more skilled performance. Thus at the outset the development of such a review process, with appropriate training, can begin to resolve the problems being experienced.

Identify a plan

Again a specific plan can now be fairly readily constructed. Short term action requires focuses on review with the managers concerned. Longer term action must focus upon developing review processes and working on leadership style.

CHAPTER 15

Preparing for managerial succession – a case study

You are a management consultant with particular expertise in helping organisations find senior managers and coping with problems of managerial succession. You have been invited to advise the Alpha organisation. The chief executive of Alpha is 62 years old. He has been chief executive for 11 years. There is general agreement that he has managed the organisation effectively as far as results are concerned. Performance has improved consistently, from an economic viewpoint, over his period of office. Yet he is now concerned about the succession when he retires.

Your initial investigations have revealed the following views of the Chief Executive, from various senior managers:

'His style is to control everything. He queries every item of spending. His emphasis is always on target, costs – all short-term reactive stuff, with little vision or planning.'

'You get memos from him, saying ' . . . dont' tell me what is good about your department, tell me what is wrong and what you are doing about it.'

'A manager who wants to win his approval will think and act short-term, cutting unnecessary spending, including long-term development. He claims never to have refused an application for development expenditure but then most people in Alpha have learnt that there is not a lot of merit in putting forward such proposals.'

'He hates committees. On taking the post he disbanded all standing committees, stating that managers would be held personally account-able for any decision taken affecting their department. Nevertheless you could always get a decision – and a fair one – from him.'

'He came from outside himself and always said that new blood was essential in the top positions. We have lost some good people in recent years because of that.'

'The qualities that make him a successful manager make it difficult for him to provide for his own succession. The personal style of manage-ment he has established requires him to remain at the top if the organisation is to work well.'

Despite the undoubted success of Alpha there is growing concern for the future. There is no real successor in sight within the organisation. Moreover, a number of major projects are under-way under the control of the chief executive which will involve Alpha in new areas of activity. One of these has required sensitive negotiations with central government in which the chief executive has played a major role.

You are required to outline an approach designed to prepare for, and then facilitate the succession of the chief executive of Alpha. In doing so you are required to consider the management style of the existing chief executive. To what extent does this management style aid or hinder your approach? Furthermore you are required to show how your approach will ensure conti-nuity of management control, future organisational effectiveness and management development. This question can be dealt with from either a public or a private sector perspective. State the perspective adopted.

ICSA, June 1986

Identify the problem

The chief executive of Alpha is 62 years old. He has been a successful chief executive for eleven years, certainly as far as results are concerned. He has presided over a period of con-sistently improved performance. He will be a hard act to follow! Yet he is now concerned about the succession when he retires. A consultant has interviewed various senior managers. From these interviews it seems clear that the chief executive has dominated the organisation. He clearly has strong views and has controlled the business firmly. He devotes considerable attention to the control of costs, budgets and performance. Moreover he believes in individual and personal accountability. There is a feeling that his leadership style has made succession particularly difficult. Senior management feel dependent upon him. Moreover he has played a key role in key projects which seem likely to loom large in the future business or the organisation.

Look for ambiguities or inconsistencies

The case comprises a paradox. Here we have a most successful chief executive on whom the organisation has come to depend. In post successfully for eleven years there seem to be no obvious internal contenders for the succession. We are told that this chief executive was originally appointed from outside the organisation and that he has often brought in people from outside to fill senior posts. So much so that some good people have left. Thus on one hand the chief executive has managed the organisation effectively. He has worked in an informal and flexible way. He has brought in senior people from outside the organisation. He has achieved growing financial success for the organisation. Yet on the other hand senior managers now appear to feel that he is indispensible to the organisation. Succession is, therefore, a key issue for the organisation.

Clarify the problem

The leader is the person who actively moulds the organisation's image, both internally and externally. The leader gives the organisation a sense of direction. A strong leader is likely to have a very significant impact on an organisation creating a 'corporate culture'. The culture in essence reflects the organisation's values. Examples include 'customer service' and 'team work' (Delta), 'financial discipline' (ITT) or 'service' (IBM). The 'culture' of Alpha appears to emphasise 'financial discipline'. The management style of the chief executive reflects a high level of concern to be successful in the tasks of management and management control. Yet the chief executive also seems to be trusted by his senior management. Certainly his style and behaviour seem to be consistent. The organisation might appoint a new chief executive from outside, or from within. Whether or not an external appointment is made there is a clear need for management development effort. The question directs our attention to developing an approach designed to facilitate managerial succession, whilst ensuring continuity of management control, future organisational effectiveness and management development. If these objectives are to be met management development is crucial. However, far more crucial would be to ensure that the senior managers interviewed develop a much more realistic view of top leadership. In particular greater understanding is needed of the complexity of a top management role. Lack of such understanding can lead to the sort of stereotyping that we can see in the case study. The role of the leader seems to be complex and full of contradictions and uncertainties. Senior managers need to learn to live with complexity, cope with conflict, adapt behaviour to the situations in which they find themselves, build up the trust and respect of their group, and practice what they preach with their own subordinates.

To be effective top leaders it seems likely that individuals will have a high tolerance for ambiguity, be good problem-solvers, particularly with unstructured problems, be self-competent, have plenty of energy, commitment and motivation and be prepared to set moderately high standards for themselves and others. Providing feedback on performance is also important.

Thus we can identify the broad aims of a management development programme *and* criteria for selecting a new chief executive. We can now proceed to identify priorities for action and programmes to achieve these objectives.

Identifying priorities

Succession of a chief executive, particularly a dominant one, can be expected to create problems. At 62, it seems likely that he has faced up to this problem in good time. Of course we do not know when he intends to go but it is reasonable to assume that he will have a year or so in post before he does so. Thus there is plenty of time to plan and implement a management development programme. This is clearly a priority. The detail of such a programme can readily be sketched out. The main principle to be adopted is that it should focus upon the on-going work of the senior managers to be involved but provide them with the opportunities to test and develop their own managerial skills.

The managerial skills to be included are identified below:

(a)   Managing tasks:
     (i)   Structuring tasks.
     (ii) Managing resources.
(b)   Influencing:
     (i)   Superiors.
     (ii)   Peers.
     (iii) Subordinates.
     (iv)   Clients, customers.
     (v)   Collaborators outside the organisation.
(c)   Strategic planning
(d)   Managing the team:
     (i)   Building the team.
     (ii)   Maintaining the team.
(e)   Managing people
     (i)   Establishing trust and co-operation.
     (ii)   Motivating and supporting.
     (iii) Communicating.
(f)   Ensuring an 'open' climate:
     (i)   Feedback.
     (ii)   Listening.
     (iii) Maintaining openness.
(g)   Leading:
     (i)   Providing clarity, direction.
     (ii)   Creating self-esteem.
     (iii) Flexibility.

Succession of a chief executive can cause anxiety and even resistance. It may well require changes to management style and corporate culture. To manage such a transition top management must be prepared to face these issues. A consultant can help with this process but the central point is that the existing chief executive must play a key role. Furthermore any management development activity must focus upon securing answers to real problems, working on the organisation's future strategy, taking full account of culture, competition, technology developments, marketing, financing product/service developments, etc.

CHAPTER 16

Creating accountability – a case study

You have recently been appointed chief executive of the Omega organisation. Your organisation is located in a large town and comprises five operating units and a head office with personnel, client service, management services and finance divisions. It employs a total of 5,000 people. The organisation has been successful in recent years. Clients report receiving good service and the financial performance of the organisation is good. The organisation has been run on centralised lines with tight financial controls applied by the Finance Division. You have concluded that a more decentralised approach to management is needed, mainly to give unit managers greater discretion. The clients served by the five operating units have different and changing needs. You feel that greater discretion will allow a more flexible response to these various needs at unit level.

One of the ways you have decided to achieve decentralisation is to decentralise the management accounting function. Each operating unit will have a management accountant responsible to the unit general manager for operational matters. The finance director will retain overall professional responsibility for the finance discipline, for financial accounting, planning and reporting. Unit management accountants will therefore report to the finance director for professional purposes but to the relevant general manager for operational purposes.

In line with these changes, the finance director has proposed a number of changes to the role of the head office of the Finance Division. In particular, he wishes to encourage a more constructive and co-operative approach by finance staff in other divisions. In the past, finance staff have identified inefficiencies in the utilisation of resources and generally called the various unit management teams to account. He wishes to move toward a more problem-solving style through which finance staff help others both to identify problems and develop solutions. As part of this, he wishes to see a change in the extent to which the Finance Division relies solely on traditional financial control techniques, often as a means of preventing change and limiting expenditure. Finally, he wishes to reduce the use of financial and accounting jargon.

These are significant organisational and professional changes. You accept the need for them and are fully committed to decentralisation. However, you are concerned about a number of issues. Write a paper for circulation to your top management colleagues covering the following issues:

1.   What are likely to be the main problems and advantages of decentralised management accounting?
2.   What measures should be adopted to support the changed professional role for the Finance Division?
3.   What actions should be taken with the top management team (the General Managers of the five operating units, and the directors of the personnel, client service, management services and finance division) in preparation for the changes?

Each part carries equal marks. Candidates may respond to the question from either a public or a private sector perspective. State the perspective adopted.

ICSA, June 1987

Case study analysis

This final case study is included to give students the chance to develop an analysis along the lines identified. In the notes that follow our concern is to identify the main issues to deal with in responding to the question. The question requires that we identify the main problems and advantages of decentralised management accounting. The pressures for centralisation or local autonomy are identified in Figs 16.1 and 16.2 for a private sector and public sector perspective.

Fig. 16.1 Private sector organisations.

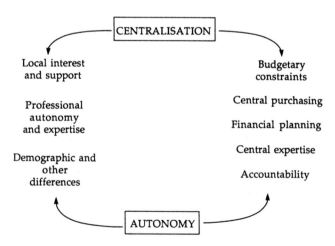

Fig. 16.2 Public sector organisations.

The question of the changing professional role creates the need for significant attitude change on the part of accountants and line managers. Partly this can be met by training but, most importantly, it requires the support and sustained effort of senior financial management. Staff must be encouraged to work co-operatively. Secondments to line departments might be considered. Project teams and working parties could be utilised. Senior financial managers must ensure that financial reports are understood. A more open style of financial management would be needed. These would be difficult changes to make. Thus the active support of top management would be essential. They must be prepared to provide the resources and the time needed. Information systems may need to be reviewed. A more open financial management style will require a constructive response from other functional managers. Any attempts to exploit a more open style for departmental advantage will lead to a rapid reversion to the previous situation. They must recognise that the changes proposed require a dramatic shift in the corporate culture. They must learn to work and to manage *as a team*. Time scales and targets must be established. A process of regular review would also be needed.

CHAPTER 17

A guide for revision and examination techniques

Examination success calls for good preparation and the application of sound examination techniques. There is no magic formula for this, just a well structured plan.

Guidelines for effective revision

- Review your work frequently throughout your course. This will save you time and mental energy when you start your revision programme.
- Look at the examination syllabus, prescribed texts and past examination papers to see what ground you need to cover in the topics.
- Find a place and time of day which *you* find comfortable to revise. Some people prefer to revise for long stretches of time, others for short bursts. Decide which you are happy with and establish this as a routine.
- Draw up a revision timetable in advance and allocate time to each subject area. Stick to your timetable as this will structure your revision.
- Find a way of organising your material in order to manage your revision. Here are some suggestions:
  1. Index cards.
  2. Subject summaries.
  3. Key words.
  4. Outline notes.
- Avoid repeated readings of large chunks of text. Read

short sections and recall them without referring to your notes. This will not help you memorise material. Follow the suggestions above. Whichever technique(s) you select, keep them short, concise and to the point.

- Practice answering questions in short time periods:
    1. List key points to be covered in answering your question.
    2. Read through key points and rank them in the order you are going to discuss them.
    3. Using your ranked list of key points expand on each in turn.
- Avoid 'burn-out' by being over anxious. Take time out in your revision programme to relax, rest and sleep.

Guidelines for examination techniques

- Read through all the questions on the examination paper, ticking any you may possibly answer. Re-read the paper carefully and thoroughly to make sure you understand the questions. Now make your final decision about which questions you will answer.
- Which should you answer first? Our recommendation is the 'examination sandwich' approach. You begin with one you are confident about, fill in the middle with others you are less confident about and finish with another confident one. Ending on a good note will make you feel more satisfied when you re-live the experience later.
- Answering the questions: as a general guide an examination question needs to *compare, contrast and criticise*. Suggested structure of your answers:
    1. The introduction should outline how you have interpreted the question and how you propose to answer it.
    2. The main body should cover key points which you then expand upon and build your argument around (as described in Guidelines For Effective Revision).
    3. The conclusion should draw together the points you have developed in the main body in summary form. *Do not* introduce new points in the conclusion.
- Make your examination script clear and neat. Examiners

mark large quantities of scripts. Speaking from personal experience, there is nothing more tedious or tiring than having to wade through a sea of bad handwriting and excessive spelling mistakes!

A final point

Examiners are not trying to trick you or 'catch you out'. They are looking for evidence that you have effectively studied and learnt from the subject and that you are capable of demonstrating that learning.

Good luck!

Index